The definition of Street Ignorance:

WHAT YOU KNOW, WHAT YOU THINK YOU KNOW, AND WHAT YOU DON'T KNOW ABOUT THE STREETS

WHEN YOU DON'T EVEN HAVE A CLUE ABOUT THE CONSEQUENCES OF STREET LIFE

BY

TERRY T. RUFFIN

DORRANCE
PUBLISHING CO
EST. 1920
PITTSBURGH, PENNSYLVANIA 15238

Dorrance Publishing Co
585 Alpha Drive
Suite 103
Pittsburgh, PA 15238
Visit our website at *www.dorrancebookstore.com*

ISBN: 978-1-6480-4308-6
eISBN: 978-1-6480-4368-0

CONTENTS

Be not over much wicked.

Neither be thou foolish

Why shouldest thou die before thy time?

Ecclesiastes 7:17

ACKNOWLEDGMENTS

If I took the time out with this pen to thank everybody that has played a part in my life to help me get where I am at today, the list would be a book itself. So if your name is not mentioned, please don't feel that I am ungrateful for the part that you played to help bring out the best in me. I hold my loyalty and my love for you deep down in my soul. I do want to say thank you to my amazing mother, Neldra Jones, and my Aunt Atsie B. Laws-Brown, who has walked with me every step of my life, through the good and the bad. I also want to say thank you to my courageous daughter, Lasheena Renee Hines, who has endured so much, but still you love so hard. I thank God for our reconciliation and new beginning.

La Rice and La' Maurie, give Granddaddy a kiss! You both give me strength. Love you more than words can express.

To my pastor, Spiritual Mother Rubell Christiani, and God Sista Tumeka White, who both have always encouraged me to know that "He that has started a good work in me, is faithful to complete it" (Philippians 1:6).

Special thanks to my cuz but more like a brother, Corey "Co-real" Moultrie, you never stopped believing in me. Just as your name, you are "real to the core." Love you, fam.

Special, special thanks to my sister and friend Maria Ervin. I know that you may be still upset with me, and I'm sorry for letting you down in the past. You seen my potential and was tired of hearing my excuses. I understand now, thank you. I love you, Sis!

And last but not least, to all of my comrades in the F.B.O.P. that helped me define who I was called to be and for giving me my new attribute, "The Good Brutha," during my incarceration in the Federal U.S.P., Canaan and F.C.I., Bennettsville. Deek, what up, loved one. Nephew J. Banks, Amen, Tally (Screwy Lou) still working them! Beloved Lee Andre White from Oakland, in the Naaaame! And my celly, D. Thomas (Tay), from A.T.L., who lent me his ear every night to hear my thoughts and ideas as I was penning this book. And to every car in the F.B.O.P., keep ya head up, soldiers, and big ups to the South Car for holding me down while I was in the trenches. My vision to be a blessing to my family, communities, and generations is now coming into full view. Never lose faith; it changes situations. One love, peace and blessings, Terry "Goodbrutha" Ruffin.

FOREWORD

THE DEFINITION OF STREET IGNORANCE

History teaches us that no society or generation has gone untouched by the elements of street life and what comes with it. Such as the lies, the hype of the fast money that's being generated by drug dealers in their own impoverished communities, senseless killings and a high mass of State and Federal incarcerations that are overwhelming the prison system with young as well as older offenders of color who have been subjected to the unconscious ignorance of the streets. I heard a man once say that fools make foolish decisions and that one foolish person can put an entire household in jeopardy. It took a long time for me to really grasp what he said. I guess the reason so was that I was a fool once myself, I knew everything but the right thing. I could dot all of the i's and cross all of the t's, I could talk that talk and had an egotistic confidence that I could walk that walk, but it was one thing that stood out about me that everyone knew but me. And that one thing was that I could not stay out of jail or prison.

Each one of my incarcerations throughout the years, I have met a lot of good men from all over the world, and all walks of life. Out of all these men, I've seen that we shared one major trait in common. We were ignorant to the philosophy of the streets.

Why? Because we would get released and end up right back where we didn't desire to be. Yeah, you guessed it! Right back in the county jail waiting for sentencing and to be shipped off to prison, whether it was State or Federal. Sometimes you come back to the system so fast that your former room that you once occupied is still open—crazy, right? But it's true and if you are reading this book and have been down that road, I know that you can relate.

Doing a bid in prison calls for you to make use of your time, during my last incarceration the lightbulb finally came on in my head. I don't know if I hit the switch accidentally or that God just got tired of seeing me wandering in the dark and flipped the switch on himself. However, it got turned on and I am grateful because it compelled me to start doing research on recidivism of repeated offenders from African- and Latino-American offenders young and old. It soon became clear to me that something more was missing. There is a saying that what you don't know won't hurt you. This saying is not only overrated but overlooked and should be overruled by the fact that what you don't know will hurt you, and what you do know can save you. And that is the reason why I wrote this book.

About the definition of street ignorance: A book about what you know, what you think you know and what you don't know about so-called street philosophy. I feel that the knowledge in this book is something that would help the generations of now and the generations that are to come understand the conspiracies to confine men and women of color young and old 16 to 80, blind, crippled, or crazy. If you live in a predominantly African-American or Latino community in the United States of America, you are a prize candidate. And being ignorant to the streets can either get you caught up in the penal system, a self-induced drug addiction, or a

          Terry T. Ruffin

violent death. That's why it's imperative that you know the truth about what really goes on in the streets.

This book for some may be looked at as an ordinary hood or urban novel, but if you are reading with an open mind and are concerned about what goes on in your community in the mind of the hustler, the mind of the addict, the mind of the offender who feels he can't do no time, and most important, the police whose mission is to get you off the streets by any means necessary. Even if it means killing you. Then this book will not only detour you from a state of street ignorance, but will also open your eyes up to the lures of the Feds and the realities and consequences of street life.

INTRODUCTION

THE GAME OF IGNORANCE

My desire for this book is to enlighten and bring awareness to the great mass of people living in African-American and Latino American communities. That are unconscious and ignorant to the tantalizing lures of street culture and unknown Federal laws that anyone who doesn't know can fall victim to. Looks are deceiving and everything that glitters ain't gold. The ideal of the streets in this modern day of time is appealing to those that have never been affected by the consequences that lies within. Overrated stereotypes such as ballers, hustlers, gangstas, pimps, stick-up kids and shooters, even the addicts and the use of some of the most dangerous drugs are highlighted and glamorized as street idols. And while these unconscious men and women play the game of street chess with their lives, there is nothing to gain but a lengthy prison sentence or a new coffin.

One thing that I noticed about the game of the streets is nothing ever changes but the street players. There is something about the streets that turns an individual's life upside down. There are no wins, only losses, and everybody that are somebodies in the streets are soon turned into nobodies. Leaving only a legacy of what used to be and how bad the episode turned out. I can almost guarantee you that the ending was from one of these three factors: addiction, prison sentence, or death. It's only one of these three that take you out of the game of street life. It's crazy because so much comes with these three factors, and I will elaborate on them sternly as you journey through this book. What urged me to put together a book concerning street ignorance was the fact that I too was a student of Streetology 101. And out of all that I have learned in class of everyday life in the streets, there was no good payoff. Only a constant self-manipulation of robbing myself from living and eating up time. Street culture has its own cultivated way of thinking and the only way to be a part of the streets you have to learn to play the game and become streetwise, and that I became. So much to a degree that in the process of learning how to be care-free and lawless, I also became a fool from the decisions that I was making. When it came to the things that I had done to people, most importantly myself, in that phase of my life running the streets. That's where the ignorantology came in at. Because had I known then what I know today, I wouldn't have went through so much turmoil, confusion, embarrassment, humiliation, obsession, and the consequences for my actions.

Being street ignorant puts you in a state of constant danger and puts your life as well as other lives in jeopardy. I have met so many individuals who wish that they could go back and replay their lives. Turning back the hands of time before that thought, choice, or decision was made that allowed them to be ignorantly committed to the prison system for life. And when I ask the question, what would be different? I always get the same response, if I knew back then what I know now, I would have never made such a poor choice or decision that caused such a calamity in my life as well as my family's life. The word ignorant means lacking knowledge or comprehension of the things specified. Now let's take a

    Terry T. Ruffin

closer look at the word ignorant, there are two key words in this definition: <u>knowledge</u> and <u>comprehension</u>.

Knowledge means the fact or condition of being aware of something and the word comprehension means the act or action of grasping with the intellect the capacity for understanding fully. The more I looked at these definitions, the more I seen that the word ignorant does not necessarily mean that a person is stupid. It simply means that sometimes we are unaware of things and situations that would lead us to damaging consequences. And it is a fact that over 98% of offenders that get caught up in the United States of America Federal prison system, never know the full debt of the price they had to be paid with time out of their own lives. And if really ignorant, the Feds have no problem with taking the rest of an offender's entire lifespan. Placing them in an insensitive system that is only concerned about one thing, and that is counting your ass three times a day, 5:30 A.M., 4:00 P.M., and 9:30 P.M. Other than that, you are just left around in a complete confusing and mindboggling system. There are so many ways you can find yourself tied to the Federal Judicial system for not being fully aware of the laws that have been set to ensnare you. Especially if you are a felon! I have met so many inmates throughout the Federal prison system that are doing a lengthy sentence because they thought the offense that they were charged with would only give them a slap on the wrist, and this is where the ignorance comes into play.

You must know that every offender that is doing time in a Federal prison could never even begin to imagine the odds that were stacked against them even at the very beginning of discovering that they have been federally indicted. The Federal System is compared to a fire-breathing dragon; its motive is to breathe hard down your back and then burn you up. I don't know where that analogy came from, but it's a good one and it best describes how one Fed charge can change an offender's life. And sometimes to the point of insanity. I wrote this book with the intentions to open your eyes up to the elements of simple unawares of the streets. That will cost you with your life as the collateral. It only takes one wrong move that would put you in the wrong place, around the wrong people, at the wrong time, and a year later you will be hit with a Federal indictment. Yeah, out of nowhere and the only question that you would be able to ask yourself is, how did this happen? Or why didn't I see this coming? Or saying the common statement that's repeated among the Federal inmate. Damn, I didn't know that my main man was a Federal informant. As I move along pouring out the ink of this pen into these pages, you will see that being ignorant to Federal entrapments of the streets is as simple as making a phone call for someone, or to someone that the Feds already have under investigation. And there you have it, you become a part of that indictment for being ignorant—crazy, right? But it's real so take your time as you read this book and remember, there is nothing fictional about the definition of street ignorance, only facts that can save you from graduating to the big boys and receiving a Federal prison number.

               Terry T. Ruffin

DEFINITIONS

COMMON WORDS USED

1.) The streets - the platform that allows the street player to generate fast illegal dollars as well as display the ignorance of their follies

2.) Street ignorance - when you don't have a clue about the consequences of street life

3.) Street players - one who engages in the actions and philosophies of street life by reason of fame, glory, or financial gain

4.) Felon - a branded street player or one who makes his way up through repeated ignorance of catching cases and qualifies quickly for a life sentence

5.) The Feds - the street player's opponent or enemy, very crafty, subtle, and moves in silence. Knows more about you than you do. Their mission is to get you off the streets for life if they can.

6.) Addictions - the use or an act of something that eventually causes the street player damaging consequences

7.) Life sentence - the common prison term that exempts the street player from the game of street life usually from his own ignorance

8.) Death - the unconscious reasoning of the street players un-awares that often leads him to this state of eternal absence from the streets

9.) You - the one that is about to read this book, wake up! Your family, your generation and your community need you. Please read with an open mind and meditate.

     Terry T. Ruffin

1

PEOPLE, PLACES, AND THINGS OF THE STREETS

CHAPTER 1

PEOPLE, PLACES, AND THINGS OF THE STREETS

> It's like a jungle sometimes, it makes me wonder
> how I keep from going under
>
> *— "The Message":*
> *Grandmaster Flash and the Furious Five*

Everyone that has some kind of dealings in the street relies on people, places, and things as a resource whether their motives are for the good or bad. Either/or, there must be some type of networking or affiliation to get a goal accomplished. People patronize different spots on the streets for different reasons, don't get me wrong, everyone that hangs in the streets are not bad people. I actually even know some individuals that have roamed in what may be considered to be hot spots on the streets, but have never been arrested for anything. For some, the streets is all they know. You have neighborhoods that had people that grew up in the midst of gangs, drugs, and violence and somehow still made a way out and have become successful. Then on the other hand, you have those that grew up in the hood, started committing illegal offenses in the hood, get caught, catch a bid, do the time, get released, then go right back to the hood or the streets to only repeat the same cycle all over again. Still whether you are a convicted felon or not you are still a candidate to be indicted, convicted, then added to the count of a Federal prison census. It's all about the choices that you make as you deal with the people, places, and things of the streets. And when people make bad choices and get caught, the Feds have a way to take something that you consider to be minor and blow it up to a full-scale high-profile case.

Prime example, if all of the drug dealers that get sentenced to the Feds are ballers, then why do 70% of these convicted drug dealers only have a locker filled with Ramen Noodle soups, if that? Why can't they afford to use the phone to call their family members? Why can't they buy Tru-links off of the computer to email as another form of communication? You know why? It's because they were never a kingpin or a large-quantity drug dealer at the beginning. The truth to this matter is that they were only street peddlers, hustling to barely get by or drug addicts selling dope to support their drug habits. Unfortunately, these offenders were with the wrong people, in the wrong place, and got caught with the wrong thing. And are now put into a position to either put up or shut up. I will elaborate more on this phase in a few chapters ahead of this book. People, places and things is what the Feds use to connect you to their sought-out conspiracies of so-called concrete evidence to indict, convict and confine you to a human warehouse in which our society calls Federal prison. It's the people, places, and things that promote probable cause to start an investigation with a valid or invalid mission to get you off the streets.

In the arena of street life people come in all sorts of flavors, it's doesn't matter what race, color, or creed. A streetwise individual normally has a lot in common with their peers in the street. Whether it be the knowledge of who is doing what, the places you can find the person doing what, or the prices, quality or quantity of what they're looking for. Put it this way, whatever it is that you are looking for in the streets, when you find the right person you will find what you're looking for. And if the person that has what

                    Terry T. Ruffin

you're looking for is moving in a state of street ignorance, that connection that you have with them may cost you tremendously. Basically, that's how it works, one man gets the next man, then the next man gets the next man and so on. This cycle has been going on for years. But the streets are so seductive and alluring that you can't see the red flags and traps that have been set, right before your eyes. The only time you will clearly see the manifestations is when you get arrested and hit with a Federal indictment. And some individuals are so street ignorant that they still miss the strategy of the opponent and get out of prison to only be an ignorant player of the streets all over again. Throughout the years, I have heard so many people in the streets say, I'm just going to hit the streets and make a quick retirement fund. Then I'm going to ride off into the sunset rich and stress free. But the truth to this matter is when you're dealing with the people, places, and things of the streets, eventually either you're going to jail, prison, or going to die. It's simple as that. Remember what I said in the beginning of this book, there are only losses. You may think that you're experiencing some wins, but I guarantee that the wins of the streets are only temporary. The most strangest thing that I've noticed about street life is that, how in the hell do you deal with a total stranger and not know his background, where he stays, the people he hangs with, his recent legal issues and most importantly if he works for the Feds as a confidential informant? Street life is filled with a lot of not knowing and taking chances and 95% of offenders that are in Federal prison are in there for taking chances. Think about it. Do you really know the people that you are dealing with in the streets? It's the same people that you hang with, eat with, sleep with, spend money on, spend money with, that will turn against you and help the Feds give you a life sentence. Yeah, you may be saying to yourself, not my people. I'm telling you and I hope that you are reading this clearly. Your own mother, father, sister, brother, wife, girlfriend, friend, homies that you grew up with from the sandbox, will turn against you in the name of the Feds. In some cases even grandmothers have helped the Federal courts give their own child a life sentence. The people that partake in illegal street activity take pride in their craft because it gives them a sense of stability, responsibility and control. But these gestures are only temporarily because being successful as an illegal street entrepreneur, is the biggest hoax or lie that has motivated African and Latino-American communities all over the United States of America. And the Federal Government only feed fuel to the flame, by flooding the communities with the so-called illegal elements for artificial bait. That's a good example, because that's how we do in our communities. The artificial bait is on the hook and everybody is chasing something, that is not real. And once that poor decision is made, the individual realizes that the eye-gleaming money-making hook that was bit, was only a fictitious fairytale. And now you are reeled in, handcuffed and thrown in jail. An analogy of the fish getting hooked, reeled in and thrown in a box of ice. And anyone of you that is reading this book knows that getting thrown in jail, is just like getting thrown in a box of ice. And the Federal Government loves to play these games of entrapment and truthfully, they are good at it.

That's why the Federal Government spends billions of taxpayers' dollars a year training the entire legal system how to strategize, institutionalize, and monopolize men and women all over the United States, that are ignorant to the streets. If you don't believe me check this out. In the criminal justice system some probation officers, becoming the lawyers, lawyers become district attorneys and district attorneys become judges, judges become politicians. In any city or state that you stay in, you will see the same group of

Terry T. Ruffin

probation officers, attorneys, district attorneys and judges fraternizing with one another. Scratching each other's back and switching out favors per client. You're facing a 20-year sentence and you have been appointed a lawyer that used to be a D.A. (District Attorney) or you have the D.A. (District Attorney) that's on your case that used to be a defendant lawyer. Now, how is it that you will go from helping a defendant to claim his innocence, to trying to convict a defendant years later? In most cases in the same court. The same thing with the judges that were once D.A.s against the defendant, are now judging some of the same defendants' cases. Another good example of the ignorance that the player of the streets partake in. The penal system is divided into two parts—common sense and ignorance—and it is always what you don't know at the beginning that eventually hurts you. Finding yourself, behind a prison wall with a lot of time and mental anguish.

The places that the players of the streets fraternize, hang out or what the system may call loitering, are normally the areas of the neighborhood or the streets that they grew up in. When I was coming up we used to call our home base setting "around the way." Nowadays they call it the hood and every hood has a name, and the people from that hood are somehow attached to that name. Not only that, any activity that goes on in that hood is well known in all of the streets. And is promoted by word of mouth to let the players know who's doing what, when, and where. Sort of like an exclusive radio commercial for all the ears of the streets. But the same way that the streets have intel of the who, what, when and where, the Feds have an ear, eye, or wire to the streets as well. It's the places that the players of the streets do their getting-money schemes or what the government calls illegal activity, that will give them a foundation to build a case on an indicted offender. Everything that the Feds does is calculated and documented. You would be surprised to know that the Feds know your own hood better than you do. Every street, every cut, every path and every fence, even down to who has dogs in their backyard. The reason so is that they want to make sure that their investigation is detailed and precise. To make sure that their findings is a clean sweep conviction of a guilty plea, or a finding of guilty by a jury that is convinced that the Feds are accurate in their investigation of your ignorance. Places of illegal activity dealings may not seem to be that big of a deal. Besides, you may have been staying and trapping (selling drugs) beside an elementary school. Or a neighbor that parks their school bus in the yard every day, when she finishes dropping the kids off from school. But what you didn't know is that once you get busted or indicted by the Feds for selling your product from out of your house or yard beside the elementary school or home with the school bus in the yard. Not only will you have to deal with the dope charge, but the school zone enhancement that will be attached to the offense as well. Actually the school zone enhancement will be the probable cause for the Feds to pick your case up from the state, if it's not Fed at the beginning. Every perimeter of the streets, the Feds have calculated by satellite. So if you got hit selling dope by a school, expect the school zone enhancement, this is one of the tactics that the Feds will use towards you to get that guilty plea. From the cellphone towers, light pole cameras, or even that mailbox that you just made that play (drug deal) by, can cause you to get that extra 10 years. Sometimes even life, whatever the case may be or how bad they want you.

Being ignorant of how you move in these places on the streets only strengthens the investigation to put you in a bad position. You call it trapping the Feds are laughing, they kick your door in, now you are trapped or entrapped in a place that you once thought you knew so well. But come to find out that someone else knew your spot better than you, and would one day be that place for you to get taken off of the streets. When you are busy running back and forth in the streets you never see these elements that are the cause and effect of a future downfall. All we see is the money, women, fame and glory, but it's important that you know that once you get hit with a Federal indictment, all of those things disappear. And you'll be left only with a hand filled with papers from the Federal courts and not even having a clue what happened. And to add to your crisis a long, long line of betrayal, from the people that you felt were on your team. And this is a reality of thousands of men of color from all over the United States, who are incarcerated in Federal prison and felt that what they were doing, would get them a tap on the hand. So watch the places that you patronize in the streets, someone may just be watching, ready to get on your line and start a new file. So far I have been putting you up on how easy it is to get caught up and bagged by the Feds by dealing with people and hanging in places that the Feds may already have people planted. Or zones that they used to enhance your sentence or create a Federal investigation.

Now I want to talk about the things of the streets that will get you caught up into a Federal indictment. The most common instrument that I have seen used as a weighty testimony for the Feds is a cellphone. Cellphones can entrap you in so many ways. Cellphones have cameras, sound recorders, social media, most important every phone has a GPS device on it. Whether you have your locator activated or not. So don't be fooled by the locator off-and-on checkbox. That signal is always on and the only way that your phone can't be located by the Feds, is if you submerge the transmitter into a sea of water. And even in that condition some models will still allow you to be located. The cellphone today has helped the Feds convict 60% of Federal offenders that get indicted. The GPS System tells the

Feds data of basically every move you make. Every call and every text is pinged, recorded and stored in a data that will recollect your everyday activities. This street ignorance of the players in the street literally kills them in a Federal Court. Because once you see how much evidence they have of your activities, you will realize that the little box (phone) that helped you make all of that dough, was your Pandora's Box that opened up the gates of hell. Another source of evidence that is frequently used to convict Federal offenders is the social media. This is something that I never understood, if you are selling dope or doing something illegal, why would you want to broadcast your business for the world to see? If this self-incriminating act is not street ignorant, I shake my head every time I hear about someone getting indicted because of this. Did you know that the Feds have agents employed just to monitor the everyday activities of social media systems? So if you and Junebug, the known neighborhood crack dealer are on Facebook or Instagram, flashing a handful of money with a pistol in your waist. It won't be long before the Feds come kicking down your door. It is the things that we utilize for our own entertainment that entrap us, the Federal Government is crafty when it comes to seeking a conviction or convictions. They don't care about who you are, who you know, or what good you have done, or even how many kids you have. Their major concern is to get you off of the streets, for as long as they can, even if it is for the rest of your lifespan. And it is the street ignorance that we have about the laws and what they can do that will allow them to do what they came to do. The streets are filled with so many fictitious philosophies, and these foolish schools of thoughts, will only lead you down a path of destruction. For what you don't know, and not trying to know will hurt you.

Terry T. Ruffin

2

STREET SENSE

SOMETIMES MAKES NO SENSE

CHAPTER 2

STREET SENSE SOMETIMES MAKES NO SENSE

> They say that common sense can cure anything
> but sense has never been common.
>
> *—Anonymous*

When I first started doing research on a lot of subjects that are highlighted chapters for this book. I began to see how everything that I wanted to discuss dealt with some form of sense whether it was book, common, or street sense. You may have just said to yourself duh, everything in life, deals with some form of sense. But truthfully, do you know that there are times that we are just going through the motions and not using or utilizing the intuitions that dwell from within? Sort of like a game that you have just put in your PlayStation console and you haven't pressed the start button yet. But what you do see on the screen of the television, is the introduction display of the game that just keeps replaying over and over again. This repetitive cycle will keep replaying over and over and over again, until you press the start game button. Once this is done you're able to actually move forward as you start playing the game. Please stay with me, I'm trying to make a point here. You see, any kind of sense doesn't work for you unless you have actually activated, or pressed the start button of awareness in your brain to put that particular sense into action. Street sense is a sense of survival and for some in utilizing it, their button is always on the go. Being street savvy or having a sense of sharpness in the streets has kept a lot of players in the game out of the court system as well as prisons. But for some reason, that sense of awareness tends to start experiencing clichés here and there. And what used to be sound judgment and always having a keen perception of what is going on around you, tends to not be effective for you as it once was. You are now taking more losses than ever, people are dropping around you like flies, either dying or going to prison. Something is telling you on the inside that you need to fall back 'cause something just ain't right. What I'm doing here is just giving you a scenario of what goes on in the average street player's mind, when the early warning signs are flashing right before their eyes. These warning signs are what I call "common sense" that we all possess trying to kick in. A lot of State and Federal offenders that are doing time or have done time can agree with this proverb: "There is always warning before destruction." And when we get so far out there mentally in the streets, we soon become ignorant and void acts and use of common sense, therefore your street sense will make no sense. I have seen some of the best hustlers in the world get caught up with Federal indictments because of moving with street sense and not common sense. A few sentences up I gave an analogy of the PlayStation game and how the screen only shows a repetitive cycle until you press start. The reason so is for you to see a good comparison of how it is when you are moving around on the streets subconsciously, and not using the intellect, or knowledge that you have to make good decisions, and that will keep you from getting entrapped in a Federal case.

The repetitive display is an example of how we think that we are conscious in the game of the streets, but when that calamity hits, we realize that all of the running, hanging, banging, and slang-

    Terry T. Ruffin

ing was just eating up time, because you never got the opportunity to press the start button in your life. You were just like a game display before pressing start, going through the motions. Street sense is a valuable asset to have when you are running the streets. But if you don't apply the common sense, then your street sense is no good. When you are not being observant of all the things and people that are around you, that's a clear sign that you have fallen asleep and moving about solely in street sense and not common sense. That would have allowed you to pick up on the small things that you cannot see on the streets. And this unawareness is basically the definition of street ignorance. Which often leads you to falling victim to a State or Federal indictment. Normally this is how it works, it's the unconscious behavior that gets you bagged. I remember when I was playing the streets hard, I would be moving so fast, roaming here and there, not even recognizing that I was entertaining unknown traps. That eventually, I found myself in a pair of handcuffs, wondering how in the hell did this happen, slowly marinating in my own ignorance. The criminal justice system monopolizes off of the ignorance of the street players. And the Federal prosecutors with a tough-on-crime mentality always use methods of the offenders' ignorance to lock them up and throw away the key.

The average person on the streets often feels that he is in control. The plays that he makes gains him reputation and street credibility. But that school of thought often vanishes to misery when he sees that it was his own activities, that cost him a lot of grief. This is why I wrote this book, to give you a clear view of how easy it is to be operating out of ignorance. When you are making all types of illegal moves, and not knowing how great the consequences may be. When it comes to what the criminal justice system considers to be a substantial amount of time that the Feds give you, and it may be your life. So the reality is that street sense is a sense that doesn't give you a good defense, from the dangers and the lawmen who lurk on the street. And street sense can save you, but if this is true, then why are the United States prison systems overcrowded with men who relied on street sense to do their business or dirty work on the streets? I hope that you can clearly see that having street sense is the equation of simply put, street ignorance which never gives a good payoff. Street ignorance is the wellspring of the criminal justice system. Without the ignorance, and unconsciousness, of the fellow street players that make up our community, every employee that constitutes our court system would be out of a job. So the prime goal is to keep you ignorant and also keep the street player's mind incarcerated. You noticed that I said mind instead of body, because if they can keep the offender's mind incarcerated, eventually the body will follow. So what I'm saying here is that street sense, is only a temporary consciousness that eventually cause you to face consequences, that sometimes will even cost you your life. Street sense is a sense that you will rarely hear the street player talk about. Because the truth to this matter is that they are unconscious of the fact that their everyday moves, and irrational thought pattern, cause them to suffer from bad decisions and criminal thinking errors. That eventually plant the offender in a Federal investigation, and put away for the rest of their lives, from their own ignorance. And displays the big picture that if you consider having street sense, as a unique sense of being street smart, when you look back on your activity or activities, you will get a good glimpse of how what you thought was a smart move, was one of the dumbest or street ignorant moves that you could ever make.

       Terry T. Ruffin

3

THE STREETS
(PREDICTABLE OR UNPREDICTABLE?)

CHAPTER 3

THE STREETS (PREDICTABLE OR UNPREDICTABLE?)

> Our greatest sorrows and most intense struggles
> emerge from places that once brought us joy.
>
> —*Author unknown*

Out of all of the chapters in this book, I really anticipated in writing and elaborating on this subject. Doing Federal time allowed me to troubleshoot and ask a lot of questions to my peers (Federal inmates) about the subject. Are the streets predictable or unpredictable? I got so much feedback and different scenarios of numerous situations for indictments that led a lot of Federal offenders to the Federal System, mostly African-Americans or Latino descendants young and old. The question is a little bit tricky. When asked most of my answers, or feedback that I got when ask the question was unpredictable. But when carefully thought out, predictable became a more suitable answer. And if you are wondering why would someone say that the streets are predictable, check this out. Every day we see, hear, read about or either experience the consequences of the streets, it's only the ignorance that motivate the street player to continue to pursue in his everyday adventures of riotous or reckless living. To the player, his mind wants to believe that nothing is going to happen. But to one that is looking from the outside in, to them it's always a predictable ending because the person that is conscious can see the ignorant moves that the street player is making on a daily basis. And when a man can't make the decision because of his ideology of what's in the streets and his fictitious fantasies of getting rich, eventually everything that he has going for him will come to ruins. The Feds love this ideal way of thinking. The most dangerous way of thinking for the street player is for him to think that he has no opponent. The Feds incarcerate thousands of men and women of color who graduated from the school of street ignorance and who wasted their lives to a system that indicts, convicts, and monopolizes off of the hard-earned funds that their family sends them, the streets are designed for you to participate in a game where there is no wins. The lifestyle of living good or balling, as some would put it, always has a bad outcome. And it's the ignorance that allows you to go through the constant confusion and havoc of everyday street life to only crap out in the end. And the first thing the offender says is I didn't know or see this coming. But the truth to this matter is that we, and I repeat we, because I was once included in this arena. We may not want to admit but we seen everything coming to an end. Because in the streets nothing lasts forever and it's always the ignorant choices that land us in a Federal prison or a coffin. The streets have a way to keep you stressed out, throwed off and irresponsible. And for someone that's reading this book that has never been incarcerated or in trouble with the law, this may be kind of hard to digest or comprehend. For those that are still playing the game of street ignorance and seem to have no idea of what I'm talking about, you haven't felt the pain of what ignorance can bring. Not wishing you no bad luck or karma, but from where I'm sitting at right now in a Federal prison dorm, at the table writing this book. I can tell you as I look around about 90% of the offenders in this dorm, were once in your shoes and the pain

Terry T. Ruffin

of being duped by ignorance may not be visible, but it is there. I am not writing this book from a psychology standpoint, because I am not a psychologist. Nor a person who has studied criminal justice. I am not a lawyer or a paralegal, I am writing this from experience and it's as raw as it gets. A Federal inmate who was once a candidate of street ignorance and was given 70 months of my life. For a law that I didn't even know existed that caused me this fate, and I will go a little deeper into my situation as you move forward into this book.

I'm in hopes that you are now beginning to see the point of how the streets are actually unpredictable to the unconsciousness of street ignorance, and predictable to the ones that's not in the streets. The word predict means to foretell on the basis of observation and experience. A short definition but very powerful and self-explanatory. In every situation of the streets, I guess it is safe to say that the outcome is predictable, because when you play in the streets it's always the same negative outcome. A lengthy prison sentence, crippling injuries, or death. But in spite of everything going on around the street player, the ignorance keeps them in a state of unpredictable circumstances. When I was playing the streets, I used a spontaneous method of going about my day. There is a saying that best describes my old logic way of thinking (T.T.G.), which means, trained to go. This way of thinking caused me to get into a lot of havoc, because I was out of control just a body moving without a functioning brain, and unconscious to every element of hinderance around me. Before you knew it, I had accumulated a criminal rap sheet with some of the dumbest offenses that you could ever think of. And now that I'm thinking about it to me there was no such thing as the unpredictable, because my behavior and lawlessness lifestyle was not only easy for me to predict. But for those around me they could see that eventually I would end up with a life sentence or laying in a casket at the funeral home. That's how ignorant that I had become with my own life, and I must say that I was one of the lucky ones to had done only a few short sentences and in the mist to figure out the damage that I was causing to my family, as well as to myself. When you're in the streets it's really about you, and no one else. You may be saying to yourself that's not true, let me elaborate a little on the "it's about me only" syndrome, so you can get what I'm saying. When you are out in the streets taking chances, and encountering all types of unhealthy situations. Not only do you put yourself in jeopardy, but you are also putting your family's lives in danger, or jeopardy as well. It's crazy how we rotate with numerous street players, or people of the street to only find out that the people you hung with on a daily basis were not loyal to you as a friend or business associate. It's your family that normally has to pick up the pieces when something happens to you. Such as coming to your court hearings, staying in touch with your lawyer, putting money on your books for your commissary. And visiting when you are housed clearly across the country. Your family are the ones that suffer when you are ignorant in the streets. It's your family that's telling you all of the time that you need to get yourself together and it's also your family that the Feds begin to communicate with first when they are starting an investigation on you. And normally it's your family that's persuading you to cooperate with the Feds to make your sentence shorter. They are most definitely seeing things from a different standpoint. They don't seem to understand your loyalty to the people that seem to not give a damn about you. They don't seem to understand how you would go to trial and face the chance of losing to a life sentence, when the Federal Government was trying to only give you 10 years with your cooperation. They just don't understand how your street ties and credibility means more to you than life itself and that you

                         Terry T. Ruffin

would rather spend the rest of your life in prison away from them than to be labeled a snitch on the streets.

The games that we play in the streets are mindboggling and it's that ignorance that keeps us from getting away from the things that are overrated in the streets and don't make any sense. That's why it's your family that suffers when you are out in the streets wilding out and going through the "it's only about me" syndrome. This is another one of my observations that I have seen from dealing with the streets and the ignorance that one embraces when their tied to it. We pay more attention to the people and things of the streets than we do our own children and loved ones and when something happens to you, they are normally the first ones that are there. Question: can you predict who will be there for you, when the walls begin to crumble around you and you find yourself sitting in a jail cell? Who will be there? Something to think about. Predictions in the street has been foretold for ages but how can one that is ignorant of the true consequences of the streets tell you what is going on around you when they don't even know themselves? The ignorant are in control of the streets and if you're following their patterns and idolizing their swagger, then eventually you'll find yourself caught up in the system fighting for your life or in a casket, not knowing all of the pain that you have left behind. The idea of this book is to get the reader to think about the big picture of what living a reckless lifestyle can manifest in your life. The greatest problem that we have in our community is that we never think. We just act and when we are living this way, your result is always going to be negative. The streets, predictable or unpredictable, is basically how you look at things. You may think that they are unpredictable, but if you are thinking this way, it is because you are taking chances in your everyday life. But you know that in the end that you will eventually face your consequences. And if your thought life allows you to see that the streets are predictable, then you are aware that ignorance plays a major role in the mentality of the streets. And that there may be a few wins for a time, but sooner or later the clock stops ticking and some new player is ready to step up in your position, continuously playing the game of ignorance.

Terry T. Ruffin

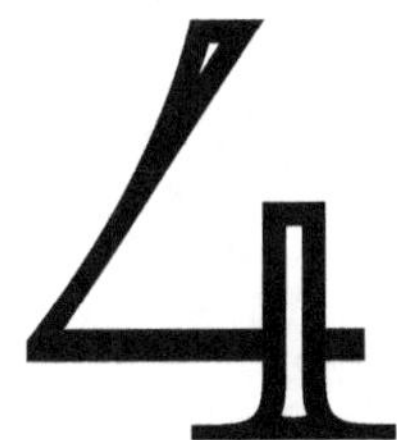

4

IF THE STREETS IS WATCHING, THEN WHO ELSE?

CHAPTER 4

IF THE STREETS IS WATCHING, THEN WHO ELSE?

I'll be fresh as hell, let the Feds watch.

—*"Feds Watching" 2 Chainz and Pharrell*

In the streets there is always a lot going on, the street players are out and about making moves and trying to make a dollar. In the process of all of the rotation going on it's almost impossible to calculate or know whose who and what everyone is up to, but one thing is for sure, someone is always watching you. This chapter is entitled "If the Streets Is Watching, then Who Else?" The reason I decided to write on the subject is because it's important for you to know that over 95% of incarcerated offenders were hit with Federal indictments because of unknown surveillance. It's crazy how we can be moving on the streets throughout the day and not even know that someone is on your line. The Feds are clever when they study you. They are taking a ignorantology course of some of the most dumbest moves that you could ever make. Once you get hit, the Feds can tell you as well as show you calculated steps of your everyday routine. From you leaving your home with your wife, or child's mother. To every move that you make in full-exposure photos, that they have taken of you in action throughout your day. The street player is usually the last person to know that the Feds are watching them. Even though street gossip normally is the channel that all participants tune in to, when it's your name on the radar, it's too late.

Everybody that rotates on the streets has some type of intel of what's going on or who is doing what. The Feds partake in this same detailed gossip. That's how they mostly put together their cases, by what they hear, then they start the investigation and go out and see for themselves. In these days and time, you never know who is watching you, especially when you are surrounded by buildings or houses. Binoculars, cameras, scopes, and cellphones play a major role in capturing criminal activity or what the Feds assume to be criminal conduct, either way if they are on your line for any reason, and have taken pictures or recordings of you, they will have a better chance of finding you guilty in a court of law. The rap song "Let the Feds Watch" by 2 Chainz and Pharrell Williams hit the airwaves in 2014. The song boasted on shining and ridiculing the Feds when they are out doing their investigation on whoever is doing what. But it's easy for you to scrutinize the Feds and their tactics when you are making millions of dollars legit or legal. The truth to this matter is whenever you get indicted, the things that once brought you joy are the same things that bring you pain. The new cars, houses, clothes, and other assets that were purchased with money from your illegal activities will become the motive for the Feds to classify you as a heavyweight drug dealer or will give you the leadership role in the crime that they label you with. All of these materialistic items will be taken away from you and given to someone else. That's how it works, no good that is gained from the streets lasts forever. We fall into the ignorance when we get consumed into things that cause us to lose track of who we are. This is a common practice for the street player. Self-entrapment is the offender's greatest enemy and it causes him to be a victim of his own

          Terry T. Ruffin

game. We can move in some of the most dangerous places of the streets and have a sense of security that everything that you do nobody knows, but the truth to this matter is that somebody is always watching. The Federal and State prison system is bursting out of the seams with men and women of color young and old from the ideology that their moves are not seen. It is imperative that you understand the seriousness of your actions and that every detail of your activities the Feds will hold it against you. Every offence has what they call a relevant conduct. It is what you do in the occupation of the crime. This relevant conduct is an action word, and it's your behavior while you are chasing that dollar that will get you a life sentence. When you're out in the streets, you live such a carefree life and that unconscious way of moving about can cost you a lot of consequences. The Feds will let you gain all of the assets that your street capital can buy, to only build a case on you, and take it right back.

The streets is appealing the limelight, the glamour, the fictitious fantasies of being all you can be, in that life. But that extravagant lifestyle soon comes to a halt and true reality exists within the courtroom and the fact that you wasted time on temporarily pleasure for a long-term pain. The Federal prison system now has a low tolerance on those that are ignorant of the law. The doors are now revolving for repeated offenders that are making the same mistakes over and over again. And truthfully no one seems to give a damn about the multitude of men of color young and old that are wasting their lives to the lies of the streets, and the tricks that the Federal Government plays on those that are ignorant of the law. I always find myself asking the question, who is the blame? What makes a man persist on bringing turmoil to himself. We all want to shine in life, one way or another. But when you are making your money moves and being flashy you're only drawing attention to yourself. Question, if you can see what everyone else is doing in the streets, what make you think that no one is watching you? The Feds have so many gadgets to take pictures of you that it is ridiculous. Gold chains with cameras on them, shirts, hats, belts. Check this out, glasses and even fake dreads (hair) with built-in cameras. These devices are normally worn by people who are close to you or your regular business partners turned into C.I.s or informants. That's why it is so easy for the Feds to get convictions because they're clever and are good at what they do. The Feds thrive on the ignorant who fall for anything, to make a quick dollar. So always remember that when you think that no one is watching, there is always someone standing somewhere looking your way and it just may be the Feds or some other cats trying to get in your pockets. I'm pretty sure you already know the odds of that reality but I'm not writing this chapter to expound on the stick-up kids, 'cause you are probably already aware of the chance of that happening. If you are out in them streets, then it is a good possibility that it just maybe somebody that is close to you trying to get that lick (your money) even if it means taking your life. The Feds want to do the same thing when they are watching you, they are trying to get a piece of your lifespan. So take my advice, don't try to be 2 Chainz or Pharrell, on some "I'll be fresh as hell," let the Feds watch. That is just one of the most ignorant ways of thinking to shine a light on your street dealings and incriminate yourself to allow the Feds to give you a life sentence. It's real and clearly a definition of street ignorance and there are plenty of street players in the Feds doing time as I'm writing this book that can vouch and agree with all I am saying.

5

STREET HUSTLING AND ADDICTIONS

CHAPTER 5

STREET HUSTLING AND ADDICTIONS

> The only thing I want to know is what you are going to do next.
>
> —*Robert Griffen III*

The streets are filled up with players that are trying to monopolize on anything that will bring in a quick dollar. The street hustler works the streets as if he is working a real job, but the hours are not nine to five, it's twenty-four hours around the clock. The hustler is consistent and committed to his or her craft, whatever product the street player is selling, the product is on demand and it gets sold just as retail does in clothing stores or outlets. You won't believe that some hustlers are so good at their game that they can sell you a match out of a matchbox. It's all about swag and lingo, when I was growing up we used to call it having the gift of gab (meaning a good persuader). I can go on all day about the cunning and crafty art of manipulation of the street hustler and the extent that one will go to to make thousands of dollars in a short time. I guess that is why the streets are so tantalizing and alluring to the street player. But what the hustler don't know is the after-effects of getting the fast money, and we all know that when you are doing something illegal, there is a price that you have to pay when you finally get caught and anything that you are doing for a long period of time, that you have to duck and hide, it's a known fact that you will get bagged eventually.

Back in the day, as long as you were not robbing banks or selling kilos, you didn't have to worry about the Feds but times have changed, the Feds are picking up everything, especially gun cases. All you have to do is have priors and get arrested with a gun possession case, the Feds can hit you with an offense called 922-G Felon in Possession of a Firearm, and if the gun is loaded, it's an automatic enhancement, which can carry a sentence of five years for each bullet. I will go further into details in the upcoming chapters about the firearm possessions and the enhancements that a firearm can bring. But the charge still ties into this chapter because the street player every now and then runs into problems and dilemmas with other street players or stick-up kids and truthfully one would rarely go without a weapon in the streets. If not in possession of one, they would most definitely know where to get one from and the guns on the streets are plentiful. And this is where the ignorance comes in as well, 'cause while you are running and ripping the streets, and having those few brushes with the law, catching those minor convictions. Doing a year here, three years there and maybe a little probation. The convictions put the street player in jeopardy because if you just so happen to get pulled over in a traffic stop, whether driving or riding with someone, and that vehicle just so happens to have a pistol inside of it. Or if that house gets raided and the Feds find weapons in that residence and you got a felony on your criminal record. There is a chance that you can end up with a Federal indictment for possession of firearm by felon. The street player takes a lot of chances while they are out in the streets trying to get paid. But in the event of the everyday struggle, the player faces so many obstacles and at the same time making so many bad decisions, that would later become detrimen-

     Terry T. Ruffin

tal to their wellbeing, especially when they end up in a Federal Court. I know that you are saying to yourself as you read this book, why does he keep mentioning what the Feds would do? My type of hustle doesn't even involve the Feds? That's what I used to think, that only small illegal actions stayed in the state courts, until I went to the Feds and seen that it was inmates doing time for all types of offenses. I have even met one young man doing his Federal sentence for stealing candy bars in a Federal jurisdiction and because he had a lengthy criminal history, he was indicted and sentence as a career criminal. The majority of street players that I've met while I was incarcerated were victims to street ignorance, it was always the same unconsciousness of their behavior and consistent inabilities to grasp all of the shady people and traps that adorned the streets. So, for the hustler it's a constant rotation of mental warfare and if one doesn't know how to think in a format to eliminate their follies. Then the ignorance would be the latter anguish, when faced with the fact of fighting for their life, for something that they thought was a petty crime.

I have also seen that a lot of the street players, that are in the game at this present time, are getting hit (arrested) as soon as they make their first piece of change. This sudden consequence comes quickly due to today's technology, it doesn't take much to slip up on a phone, camera, or wilding out when your high or intoxicated. That's why I also added the word addictions to this chapter. Because addiction plays a major role to disaster, to the street player. The word addiction means a compulsive need for and use of a habit-forming substance. Over 70% of the street players in the United States are challenged with some form of drug addiction, whether it's marijuana or other high-potent lethal drugs, all drugs alter the street player's mind and detour him or her from common sense. When you are being motivated or controlled by mind-alter-ing substances it's hard for you to comprehend what's going on around you and the faltered moves that you are making throughout your daily routine. Addictions and hustling don't match up, most of the addicts or chronic drug users I've seen throughout the years were once major players in the game, to only slowly fall off due to catastrophes of their drug use. It is easy for an addict who has gone habitual, to get entangled in a Federal investigation. The Feds know that the average street hustler and addict has a lengthy criminal history, and will use that tactic to put them in a position that their backs are against the wall. Normally when this happens, it's a known common fact that a good percent of drug addicts and I think that it is safe to say as well, street players or hustlers, become C.I.s (confidential informants). Not all but a great percentage, and the Feds have them planted in communities all over the United States. The Feds will let their C.I.s possess drugs and in some cases guns, for the purpose of fulfilling their investigation. Who are the confidential informants? It could be anybody that's involved in the street life, and most of those Federal informants turned out to be the people who are close to you. It's no need to act surprised about what I just said. Look at the high-profile cases that often hit the media, and look who the witnesses are. Yep, you guessed it. It's the people that's close to you that seals your fate in the Feds. Street hustling and drug addiction to the street player commonly goes hand in hand, in our communities today. The hustler frequently uses what the media considers today as recreational drugs in which they become codependent on and often using the drugs as a coping mechanism to deal with a heavy stress and strain of the streets.

Check this out. The Feds even give you points concerning your classification if you used drugs prior to your incarceration. Along with a sentence guideline system that goes sky high with your

 Terry T. Ruffin

points if you got a prior criminal history and the use of drugs. So remember that everything you do today with your criminal lifestyle will affect you tomorrow or the years to come, if you catch a Fed charge. So don't be ignorant about making moves in the streets, hustling or being carefree in drug addictions, 'cause the Feds will most definitely use your reckless behavior against you. Running the streets making illegal moves and staying high all of the time will only lead you into a trap. I'm not saying that this is always the case, but it is better to be safe than sorry, 'cause once the Feds get on your line, it's hard to shake them. And if you're out in the streets hustling and battling drug addiction, at the same time, then there is a chance that you just may serve the wrong one and there you have it. A Federal case that you have to deal with your past and present ignorance.

6

THE PROSPERITY AND POVERTY OF THE STREETS

CHAPTER 6

THE PROSPERITY AND POVERTY OF THE STREETS

> A little sleep, a little slumber, a little folding of the hands to rest; so shall your poverty come like a prowler and your need like an armed man.
>
> *—Proverbs 24:33-34*

Every street player that is attached to the street life has one major goal in common. And that is to get money, and it's a lot of cash flow that generates in the streets, through illegal trade and bargaining. That's why to the street player the streets is an important factor in their lives, because that's where the bread and butter comes from to provide a life which seems fitting, comfortable, and burden free. But everything that glitters ain't gold. The street life is filled with a lot of self-gain, fictitious pleasures that tend to overwhelm the ones that partake in it, with a lot of greed and unfulfilled wants. The more money you get, the more you want, the more you want, the more chances you take, the greater the consequence, which is either a life sentence in a State or Federal prison or death of some form of violence. For the love of money, people would basically do anything. For the street player, chasing money, or becoming rich is their greatest desire and for some, there is no discretion on how they go about getting it. That ideal is what makes the streets dangerous. The greed, fictitious fame, and the influence of the ignorant keep the gutter mentality flowing throughout impoverished communities of African-Americans as well as Latino-Americans, all over the United States. It's the money that motivates the street player, and is the center of everything around them. Not only around the street players but money somehow affects the entire community.

It's because of money and the ignorance of the street player that crime runs rampant in our communities like a wildfire burning down a forest. And this is the sole reason the Feds set up shop in communities that have a high percentage of crime and senseless killings. The Feds know that where there is illegal drug activity going on, there are guns circulating, and where there are guns circulating, there are all types of crimes being committed from robberies to murders. And the majority of participants that are committing the crimes are black males and can't forget to mention are felons or have had some type of dealings with the criminal court system. I'm not trying to sound bias by any means but these are the statistics, and as I look around the dorm in a compound of the Federal prison that I am housed at, as I'm writing this chapter and can't forget to mention seeing the behavior of the average offender of color here. I must say that the current statistics on black-on-black crime and homicides are true. The Feds really are not concerned about who is dying in the streets or what dealers are getting robbed. They are in the game to only focus on the ignorance that the street player projects. It's this ignorance that keeps the Federal agents employed. It's the ignorance that allows them to incarcerate or put on Federal probation millions of men of color all over the United States a year. It's the ignorance that thousands of Federal offenders of color are released from prison to only return before the year is out, sometimes a great majority don't even make it out of the halfway house.

It's this ignorance that the Federal government thrives to produce and create strategies to get you off the streets. It is so easy to

Terry T. Ruffin

get caught up in the limelight of the streets and be blinded with the fast money, flashy jewelry, fancy cars and being able to live in a nice home fully furnished. Truthfully, who wouldn't want to have these things? There's a difference when you have bought these assets with funds that you work hard for. This type of prosperity is granted from diligence and hard work, but when your so-called prosperity comes from an illegal activity, everything and I repeat everything is in jeopardy of getting taken away from you, and the Feds don't mind you accumulating your materialistic trophies to only confiscate your winnings later on. The prosperity of the streets is what draws the street player in and they build their philosophy on the notion that the quick and easy money will be their escape from the true realities of life of hard-earned work and everyday responsibilities. Being rich in the game of illegal activities is the biggest illusion that has ever entered the mind of the African- or Latino-American, and the Feds take this myth to use against this ethnic of people to basically destroy them from their own ignorance. But once this reality sinks in, and the street player sees that he was bamboozled by a fantasy that didn't even exist. Among other things such as the fake friends, unfaithful partners, and the disloyalty of the homies that get on the stand and point fingers at you. Now the game changes from the once prosperity atmosphere, to the arena of poverty. The word poverty means, a state of being inferior in the quality or insufficient in amount. Street poverty doesn't mean that you're broke financially, it only means the shine that you once had is now blemished with heartache, mental distress, fear of the unknown and maybe a new status of becoming a lifer, in the Federal System. This poverty is one that's the lowest of the low, 'cause now the pain of reality will set in, and you will see a replay of all the ignorant moves that you have been making, and how it appears that the entire world is against you. You will begin to realize how everyone that you thought were with you, are now nowhere to be found. You'll see how close loved ones abandon you. And most importantly, how the Feds will try to take your life and turn it upside down with the lies, the enhancements, your past criminal history that sometimes will go back five, ten, to fifteen years and they will even try to use that against you. Every offender that has been hit with a Federal indictment experiences these realities, and it is crazy how all of these challenges are so evident in everyone that has had a bout with the Federal Court system, and won't even express the importance of being awoke to the entrapments of the Feds. To their family, friends, or people in the community, that they see walking in the same shoes, that they once occupied. Most offenders will do 10 years in the Federal prison system, to only get released, and fall victim again to their own ignorance, and end up going back to Federal prison. At the end of the day, the lifestyle of street ignorance is a fool's game because you don't gain anything out of the imaginary way of life, and the Federal government only uses this weakness to enhance and create more laws to suppress and oppress the men and women of color who are ignorant to the laws and to the Fed's entrapments. The entire truth to this chapter is, there is really no prosperity when it comes to getting paid doing illegal activity. Only the poverty that you experience, when them folks get into your business, and try to put your back against the wall to cooperate, and put them in somebody else's business. And really that's the only thing that appeases them. You helping them out and copping out to whatever they offer you as a plea bargain, it's their way or no way.

   Terry T. Ruffin

7
PRIORS AND CONVICTIONS

CHAPTER 7

PRIORS AND CONVICTIONS
YOUR STREET CREDIBILITY, IT ALL ADDS UP

> To do the same thing over and over again is not the only boredom: it is to be controlled by rather than to control what you do.
>
> —*Heraclitus*

So far we have covered the typical swag and unconscious behavior of the average street player, and how what he doesn't know causes him to be entrapped by his own best thinking. Street ignorance is the number-one killer among African- and Latino-Americans, because it's the ignorance that allows the street player to suffer from the unknown elements of the streets such as violence, drug addiction, lengthy prison sentences and sometimes death which is statistically high in African-American communities all over the United States. I dibbed and dabbed with the importance of street awareness, the effects of unconsciousness, and being ignorant of the state and Federal laws that are put in place to enslave you. As spoken in the Constitution of the United States, which states in Amendment XIII Section 1 that neither slavery nor involuntary servitude, except as a punishment for a crime where of the party shall have duly convicted, shall exist within the United States, or any place subject to their jurisdiction. If you did not know that once you get convicted of a felony and sent to prison you have legally become a slave to the United States. Now you do. And for the people that are conscious and aware of this factor such as the politicians, and the people that fight hard to enforce the laws that keep the people of color oppressed. They will know that this amendment in their eyes is called modern-day slavery. And they also know that the United States prison system is one of the biggest franchises in America, which monopolizes off of prison labor and controlling poor people, who are ignorant to the laws of the land. This is another one of the reasons that I was compelled to write this book, because so many of us men of color are wasting so much valuable time chasing frivolous and shallow materialistic things, that only add up to nothing. Because you can't enjoy anything that you have gained through illegal activity, once they lock you up, and throw away the key. You can't utilize anything caught up in the system. You can't be a good father to your kids, and basically you can't contribute physically, to any good relationships that you once had. It is almost impossible to stay connected to the people that you love and care about in society. And as the years began to pass while you are incarcerated, people that you once knew will begin to drop away like the leaves of a tree in the fall. If you have ever been incarcerated you should understand clearly what I am saying, but if you haven't been in that predicament brace yourself for these consequences as an end result from your street ignorance.

I remember when I was in my teens, my ignorance of the true realities around me allowed me to fall into alcohol and drug addiction at an early age. In which I can say today, became a coping mechanism to deal with unpleasant emotions. I went through a mental fog from the ages of 15 to 25. Drugs and alcohol contributed to this factor, but I also know now that my own irrational and criminal thinking played a major role with my own stability as well. I caught my first felony protecting myself at the age of six-

                        Terry T. Ruffin

teen, from a high school bully in which I had many due to my height and size. I was considered to be a little guy back then. Anyway, I was threatened by him a few times throughout the week, so I had a bag of pencils and pens in my backpack. I took a cylinder shape, rock that I found on the ground and put it inside the pencil and pen bag. This would be my protection if anyone would try to mess with me. One afternoon as I was getting off of my school bus I seen that my bully had already gotten off. But instead of him going about his way he threw his bookbag on the ground and caught eye to eye with me, as I was getting ready to step down from the bus to the ground. I always kept the rock and bag of pencils inside of my bomber jacket. In a slip hole that I had cut there to use to steal candy bars and any other thing that I could put my hands on back then. But anyway, as I was getting off the bus, the bully grabbed me by the neck and lifted me off of my feet. All of the other kids at my bus stop were chanting and yelling. I was scared to death, somehow I reached inside of my jacket and pulled out the bag, swinging it with all of my might. I must have blacked out because when I came to everyone was running away and the bully was lying on the ground with a stream of blood running down his face. I took off and sprinted home as fast as I could. The next day, I was called to the principal's office and was handcuffed by two sheriffs and was escorted out of the school with the introduction to my first felony. Assault with a deadly weapon with intent to inflict serious injury. I received in court a one-year suspended sentence for five years' probation, in which I eventually violated and did a few months in a medium-custody facility. To only get released to repeat the same cycle over again and again. As I think about it today, the bully was twice my size, I just wanted him to leave me alone and through his pestering conduct. I was the one that fell victim to street ignorance and caught a felony that would follow me for the rest of my life. I'm not justifying that what I did was right, at this stage in my life I feel that I did what any other adolescent would have done to protect themselves.

As for the bully he suffered from only a minor scratch, which probably came from the prick of the pencils. And a year later the bully and I became good friends. Not to mention one of my weed-smoking partners in which we smoked religiously every day on our way to high school. And even though our relationship changed for the better, the felony never left my criminal record. And it counted towards every criminal court situation that I ever faced. No matter how long that was ago that felony still remains just as strong as it was the day that I received it. This is the reason why I chose to use this example for this chapter, because it was the first felony that I ever caught at a tender age of ignorance that the Feds tried to use to career me out to a 15-year-to-life sentence 20 something odd years later. For a case that according to my guidelines, I could get no more than 30 months. Priors and convictions is what allows the Federal Court system to slap you with outlandish prison sentences. And the way that they rock, if you got a lengthy criminal record they (the Feds) can roll and ball you up like a piece of clay. That's a good analogy of how the Feds work, even in some cases all they needed for the offender to have was two felonies on their record and they (the Feds) balled them up as well. The Federal Court system classifies all court cases by the offender's characteristics. They do a full investigative report on each offender. And the majority of the time, once indicted they already know who you are, what you are about and number-one uno your criminal history. And where your points will fall under the sentencing guidelines. To a law enforcer having priors is all they need to know about you to justify their means of going after you to get a conviction. Even if they have no evidence the priors is a motive

      Terry T. Ruffin

for a jury of 12 to convict an offender. Your past criminal history can consist of some of the most petty charges and conduct. If you have pleaded guilty and it is a felony, it still goes on your record and it is weighty. It don't matter if the charge was nonviolent or you threw a rock and busted Ms. Taylor's window and she pressed charges on you. Didn't bring your girlfriend's car back on time and she got mad and pressed charges, and you were charged with unauthorized use of a motor vehicle. If the District Attorney is not willing to throw the charge out when your girl is no longer upset with you, you will have that felony on your record if found guilty. And it's that same felony that years later down the line the Feds will use to career you out. Normally a 10- to 15-year more sentence than your regular guidelines would call for. To the Feds, priors and convictions are the same, and what you have done in the past is all they need to turn you into a villain.

The street player experience a lot of brushes with the law and those simple or petty brushes is literally what takes them off of the streets for a long period of time once he is indicted. There is a myth among young street players that has been the greatest lie of the streets ever told, and that is that going to jail makes you a man and gives you street credibility. This myth is being accommodated throughout urban communities in the United States on a daily basis and that thought and cycle of recidivism only fuels the street ignorant in our neighborhoods. The Feds don't mind you hustling, robbing, stealing, or selling dope. They know that eventually you will slip up and fall right where they expected you to, in their grasp. And with the past criminal history that you already have, you really don't have too much to fight with in a Federal Court system.

Most offenders find themselves with their backs against the wall and give in because of the pressure and stress of how much time the Feds are offering or want to give for the charge. And once they fold or are broken they become a witness or Federal informant. It's a proven fact, throughout the system and it's the offender's priors, or past criminal history, that causes this type of reverse psychology to go from a hardcore criminal, or street player, to cooperating with the Feds about what's going on in the streets.

So if you're running the streets, and catching all types of charges and convictions. Always remember that in the game of ignorance what you did yesterday, today, and tomorrow will add up. And you can find yourself labeled as a career offender having to fight the courts for your life because of priors and convictions that you have already done time for.

 Terry T. Ruffin

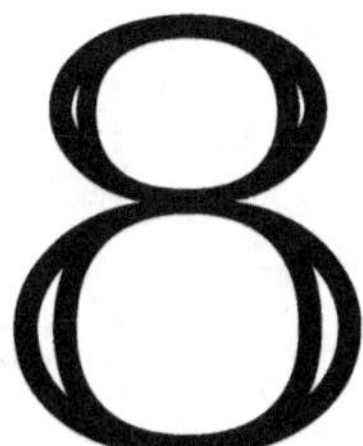

8

GUNS AND FEDERAL GUIDELINES
GIVE AN IGNORANT FELON A LOT OF TIME

CHAPTER 8

GUNS AND FEDERAL GUIDELINES GIVE
AN IGNORANT FELON A LOT OF TIME

Are you using your brain today or is it using you?

—Dr. Rudy Tanzi

In the eyes of some of the street players, possessing a firearm is the epitome of street life. Nowadays, it's kind of hard to find anyone that is about that life without one. And the Feds know this fact and they use this theory of the street player's ignorance to fill the Federal prison system to its capacity. With felons that were arrested and indicted for possession of firearm, which has now become a Federal offense. Federal law prohibits any felon (meaning a person who has been convicted of a crime punishable more than a year in prison) from possessing a firearm 18 U.S.C. 922 (g) a person who violates that restriction can be sentenced to prison for up to 10 (ten years) in Federal prison. It is this law that is causing the Feds to swarm the communities in which predominantly black men of all ages are getting arrested and indicted for having a firearm in their possession. Or in an area in which they can put their hands on it. Whether the gun is on their person, or hand reach, the Feds can take this charge and turn it into a Federal offense. And the statistics show that the Feds are picking up more than 55% of gun cases, especially if drugs, gangs, and robberies are involved.

There are so many Federal sentence enhancements that the Federal District Attorneys can relate to your case. Every offender is placed in a different category according to your Federal guidelines and what enhancements apply to you. Once the street player is indicted by the Feds the offender will find themselves, not only having to deal with a gun possession charge, but various entities of sentence enhancements in relations to that single gun charge. What I'm saying is that the Feds are harder on felons in possession of a firearm, than a non-felon who gets pulled over with a truckload of illegal weapons. The street player who is ignorant to the Federal gun laws easily falls subjected to the 18 U.S.C. 922 (g) offense. And finds themselves faced in front of a Federal Court judge, a United States District Attorney, who's on their line. And an appointed public defender, whose language may appear to be sarcastic, confusing, and combative. As if they're fighting against you and not for you. For the common street player that is ignorant to the law, their rights, and that is scared to death, their first Federal offense has their mind boggled. But normally plays along with their public defender hoping to get a good deal.

A felon in possession of a firearm is serious in a Federal Court and just being in possession of one gun can get you caught up in the Feds game. And believe me when I say this, they are ready, willing and able to play. The Feds have a 98% conviction rate. It has been this way since the Federal Government was indicting mobsters back in the 1930s. The Feds were pressing some of the most dangerous criminals in the world with threats and outlandish prison sentences to get guilty convictions. And we are now in the 21st century, close to 100 years from when President J. Edgar Hoover declared the new criminal justice system in which we call today the

     Terry T. Ruffin

Federal Bureau of Investigations. And nothing has changed with the Feds since that era. Their tactics are manipulative, conniving, and piercing to an offender's soul and from what I have seen inside the belly of the beast (the Federal prison system) the 98% conviction rate is most definitely accurate. And for those that have taken chances to fight the Federal Government to maintain their innocence. Some of these former street players are still behind the prison walls. Either still fighting for their freedom, given up from the hard-pressed battle against the wiles of the Federal Court system, or died from terminal diseases, loss of hope or a broken heart. The Federal Government now targets impoverished communities with the political excuse of cleaning up the drug-ridden and violent neighborhoods to make the community safer. But for every five guns they take out of the community, that's five fathers, sons, mothers, or daughters that's getting taken out of the community as well and subject to gun laws that will take them off of the streets for either five, ten, fifteen years or either life. This cycle is present and is going on as I am writing this chapter.

Street ignorance to the Federal gun laws is the number-one enemy to the street player. And you don't need to get caught up with a few kilos of cocaine to graduate from State prison to Federal prison. All you need to get caught with is a firearm and have a criminal record with a few felonies and you'll find yourself in a fight for your life, all over a pistol. It doesn't even matter if the gun doesn't shoot, it can be an antique pistol or rifle from the 1800s. All the weapon needs to have is a firing pin inside the trigger contraption. I have even met some offenders while I was in Federal prison who were incarcerated for being in possession of a high-powered BB gun during a robbery. And they were charged with a 922 (g) offense. Today, four out of every five homicides in the United States are committed by a gun. In urban neighborhoods the statistics are high on black-on-black crime. Meaning African-Americans being the offender and the victims. We hear it all of the time stop the senseless killings, stop the violence, but no one is talking about how it takes a willing hand to pick up a pistol to shoot and kill someone. A crazy thing about these scenarios are that once a young man kills another, that individual that done the shooting really doesn't even know or understand why he just committed such a cruel act. His true reality sets in as he realizes that he just graduated to a world that his entire environment will be controlled for the rest of his life. He has now become a victim of his own ignorance. And what he thought was disrespect from his victim, and what the streets would call a violation, he would soon come to find that all of the foolish sense of pride and street credibility politics was a bunch of crap and he now has to suffer among his peers that has also been duped by this philosophy of ignorance. Truthfully a man handles his beefs and quarrels like a man. When I was growing up, we used our hands and once it was over, it was over, and sometimes eventually became mutual friends again. How do you kill a human being or gun down your own people in the streets and don't even have a clue about why you did it?

Check this out, the Feds don't care nothing about the homicide you committed. What they do care about is that you used a gun to commit the crime, therefore after the State finishes with you, as you complete your homicide sentence, if it's not life, then the Feds will come and get you to start your Federal sentence for being in possession of a firearm. And if you got a lot of priors, they can Arm Career Criminal Act you out. I will talk more about this serious enhancement in the upcoming chapters.

So if you like playing with them guns and you got priors, don't be ignorant to the devices and schemes of the Federal government. A gun can get you a life sentence and you don't even have to pull

         Terry T. Ruffin

the trigger. This is the way they got it set up now. Even if you are riding with your brother and he has a registered weapon, if he gets pulled over and the gun is in an open area that you can reach out your hand and grab it at any time. You are liable to be in violation and be charged with possession of firearm by felon. So don't think if you get pulled over in Junebug's car and they find a pistol under the seat of his car that you can't get charged with it. If it's in the car and you can reach it, then to the police and Feds, it's yours or you know something about it being there. Believe me, this is what the definition of street ignorance is all about, to pull you up on true facts about the so-called legal system and how common sense can save you from the ignorant gestures of not knowing how the Feds work. And what can get you a lot of time for something you thought was minor. It may be to you, but to the Feds traffic tickets count when they are adding up your criminal points for sentencing purposes.

I. POSSESSION OR RECEIPT OF A FIREARM OR AMMUNITION BY A PROHIBITED PERSON

18 U.S.C. § 922(g) & (n). Punishable by up to 10 years imprisonment. May receive minimum sentence of 15 years without parole if the felon has 3 or more prior convictions for a felony crime of violence (e.g. burglary, robbery, assault, possession of offensive weapons) and/or drug trafficking felony (18 U.S.C. § 924(e))

Elements

A. Possession or receipt of a firearm or ammunition;
B. By a person who falls in one of the following categories:

- **Convicted of a crime punishable by imprisonment for a term exceeding one year** (persons under indictment or information for such a crime are prohibited from receiving firearms or ammunition);
- **Fugitive from Justice** (requires interstate flight to avoid prosecution or testimony in a criminal case);
- **Drug Users or Addicts** (May be shown by recent conviction for use, recent possession of drugs, or recent arrest for use of drugs, or positive drug tests);
- **Aliens illegally or unlawfully within the US or those lawfully admitted in non-immigrant status** (i.e. aliens without permanent residence status).
- **Mental defectives or persons committed to a mental institution;**
- **Formally renounced US citizenship;**
- **Dishonorably discharged from the military;**
- **Subject to a court order prohibiting harassing, stalking, or threatening of an intimate partner or child of an intimate partner, or placing such persons in reasonable fear of bodily injury.** (The order must have been issued after a hearing for which the person had notice and an opportunity to participate, and the order must either find a credible threat to the intimate partner or child, or by explicit terms prohibit the use, attempted use or threatened use of physical force.)
- **Convicted of a misdemeanor crime of domestic violence** (need not be classified as "domestic" crime as long as offense involves the use or attempted use of physical force, or the threatened use of a deadly weapon committed by a current or former spouse, parent, or guardian. The subject must have had counsel and a jury trial (if applicable) unless those rights were waived.)

C. The firearm or ammunition was transported at any time across a State line or from a foreign country.

II. KNOWINGLY SELL, GIVE, OR OTHERWISE DISPOSE OF ANY FIREARM OR AMMUNITION TO ANY PERSON WHO FALLS WITHIN ONE OF THE ABOVE CATEGORIES

18 U.S.C. § 922(d). Punishable by up to 10 years imprisonment.

III. USE OR CARRY A FIREARM DURING OR IN RELATION TO, OR POSSESS A FIREARM IN FURTHERANCE OF, A DRUG TRAFFICKING CRIME OR FEDERAL CRIME OF VIOLENCE

18 U.S.C. § 924(c). Punishment ranges from a minimum of 5 years to life imprisonment, without parole, or death if death results from the use of a firearm. Sentence must be served consecutive to any other sentence. Mandatory minimum sentence increases depending on: the type of firearm involved (e.g. machinegun), whether the gun was possessed, brandished, or discharged, and prior convictions under this section.

Terry T. Ruffin

IV.   STOLEN FIREARMS AND AMMUNITION

18 U.S.C. § 922(j). Prohibits the receipt, possession, concealment, storage, bartering, selling, or disposing of stolen firearms and ammunition knowing or having reason to believe the firearm or ammunition is stolen. Punishable by up to 10 years.

18 U.S.C. § 922(u). Prohibits stealing or unlawfully taking away firearms from the business inventory of a Federal firearms licensee. Punishable by up to 5 years.

18 U.S.C. § 924(l). Prohibits stealing a firearm which has moved in commerce. Punishable by up to 10 years.

V.   FIREARM IN A SCHOOL ZONE

18 U.S.C. § 922(q). Except as authorized, may not possess or discharge a firearm in a school zone. Punishable by up to 5 years imprisonment.

VI.   UNLAWFUL POSSESSION MANUFACTURE OR TRANSFER OF CERTAIN FIREARMS AND DEVICES

18 U.S.C. § 922(k) makes it unlawful to transport, ship, receive or possess a firearm with the manufacturer's serial number obliterated, removed or altered. Punishable by up to 5 years imprisonment.

18 U.S.C. § 922(o) makes it unlawful to possess or transfer a machinegun. Punishable by up to 10 years imprisonment.

18 U.S.C. § 922(v) makes it unlawful to manufacture, transfer or possess a semi-automatic assault weapon manufactured after September 13, 1994. Punishable by up to 5 years imprisonment.

18 U.S.C. § 922(w) makes it unlawful to transfer or possess a large capacity ammunition feeding device (holding more than 10 rounds) manufactured after September 13, 1994. Punishable by up to 5 years.

26 U.S.C. §§ 5861(d) and (f) make it unlawful to possess or make a machinegun, sawed-off shotgun, sawed-off rifle, silencer or destructive device without registration. Punishable by up to 10 years.

VII.   SELL, DELIVER OR TRANSFER TO JUVENILE

18 U.S.C. § 922(b)(1) prohibits a Federal firearms licensee from selling or delivering a firearm or ammunition to a person under 18, and prohibits selling or delivering a firearm other than a shotgun or rifle, or ammunition other than for a shotgun or rifle, to any person under 21. Punishable by up to 5 years.

18 U.S.C. § 922(x) makes it unlawful, with exceptions, to sell, deliver or transfer a handgun, or ammunition suitable for handguns only, to a juvenile (person less than 18 years of age). Punishable by up to 1 year imprisonment.

VIII. FORFEITURE OF FIREARMS AND AMMUNITION

18 U.S.C. § 924(d) authorizes the seizure and forfeiture of firearms and ammunition involved in or used in a violation of Federal criminal law. However, strict time limitations are imposed upon the forfeiture of firearms and ammunition

Fiscal Year 2018

▶ In FY 2018, 69,425 cases were reported to the U.S. Sentencing Commission.

▶ Of these cases, 6,719 involved convictions under 18 U.S.C. § 922(g).

▶ 18 U.S.C. § 922(g) prohibits certain persons from shipping, transporting, possessing, or receiving a firearm or ammunition while subject to a prohibition from doing so, most commonly because of a prior conviction for a felony offense.

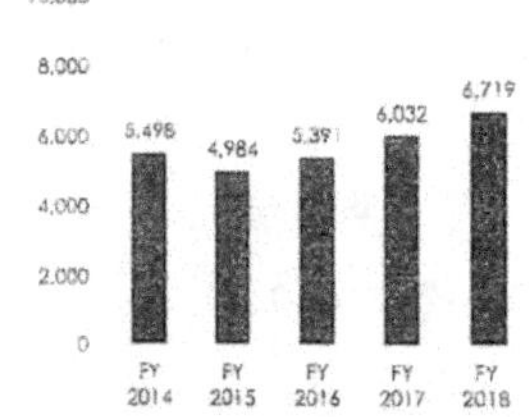

Number of Felon in Possession of a Firearm Offenders

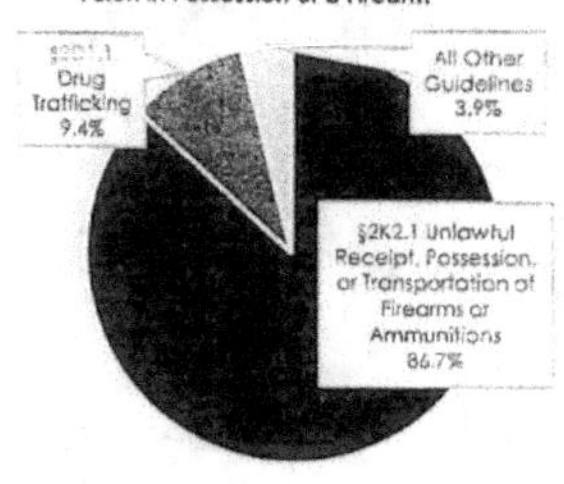

Primary Sentencing Guideline Felon in Possession of a Firearm

Offender and Offense Characteristics

- 97.7% of felon in possession of a firearm offenders were men.

- 54.2% were Black, 24.9% were White, 17.9% were Hispanic, and 3.0% were Other races.

- Their average age was 34 years.

- 94.5% were United States citizens.

- 25.6% were in the highest Criminal History Category (Criminal History Category VI):
  - 8.9% were CHC I;
  - 9.1% were CHC II;
  - 21.2% were CHC III;
  - 20.4% were CHC IV;
  - 14.9% were CHC V.

- The top five districts for felon in possession of a firearm offenders were:
  - Eastern District of Missouri (281);
  - Western District of Texas (233);
  - District of South Carolina (230);
  - Northern District of Texas (209);
  - Western District of Missouri (205).

- Districts with the highest proportion of felon in possession of a firearm cases were:
  - Western District of Tennessee (39.4%);
  - Southern District of Alabama (36.0%);
  - Eastern District of Missouri (33.8%);
  - Northern District of Alabama (32.5%);
  - Middle District of North Carolina (28.2%).

Punishment

- 97.6% of felon in possession of a firearm offenders were sentenced to prison; sentences varied widely by whether a mandatory minimum penalty applied in the case.

- 14.8% of felon in possession of a firearm offenders were convicted of one or more statutes with a mandatory minimum penalty:
  - 4.3% were sentenced under the Armed Career Criminal Act (ACCA) (18 U.S.C. § 924(e));
  - 5.0% were convicted of violating 18 U.S.C. § 924(c);
  - 5.4% were convicted of another statute carrying a mandatory minimum penalty, most of which were drug offenses.

Terry T. Ruffin

Punishment

- The average sentence for all felon in possession of a firearm offenders was 64 months.

  - The average sentence for offenders convicted of violating only section 922(g) and under ACCA was 186 months.

  - The average sentence for offenders convicted of violating only section 922(g) but not sentenced under ACCA was 59 months.

Sentences Relative to the Guideline Range

- 67.8% of felon in possession of a firearm offenders were sentenced under the *Guidelines Manual*; of those offenders:

  - 82.6% were sentenced within the guideline range.

  - 10.0% received a substantial assistance departure.
    - Their average sentence reduction was 44.5%.

  - 6.2% received some other downward departure.
    - Their average sentence reduction was 34.7%.

- 30.2% received a variance; of those offenders:

  - 88.1% received a below range variance.
    - Their average sentence reduction was 34.2%.

  - 11.9% received an above range variance.
    - Their average sentence increase was 48.2%.

- The average guideline minimum and sentence for felon in possession of a firearm offenses has declined over the past five years.

  - The average guideline minimum was 72 months in fiscal year 2018, down from 81 months in fiscal year 2014.

  - The average sentence was 64 months in fiscal year 2018, down from 72 months in fiscal year 2014.

Sentence Imposed Relative to the Guideline Range FY 2018

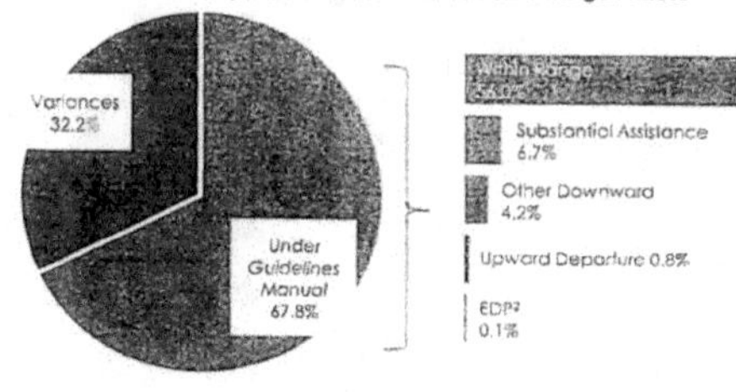

Sentence Relative to the Guideline Range (%)

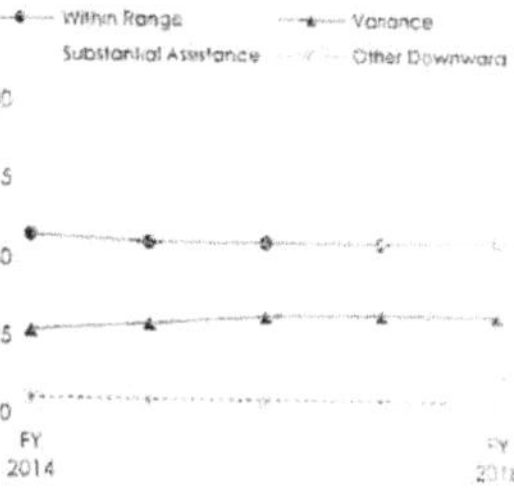

Average Guideline Minimum and Average Sentence (months)

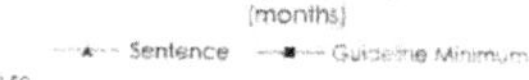

[1] 18 U.S.C. § 924(e) requires a 15-year mandatory minimum penalty be imposed on offenders convicted of violating section 922(g) with three previous convictions for a violent felony or serious drug crime.

[2] "Early Disposition Program (or EDP) departures" are departures where the government sought a sentence below the guideline range because the defendant participated in the government's Early Disposition Program, through which cases are resolved in an expedited manner. See USSG §5K3.1.

9

THE CONSTRUCTIVE POSSESSION OF A FIREARM LAW WAS DESIGNED FOR THE STREET IGNORANT; HERE'S WHY

CHAPTER 9

THE CONSTRUCTIVE POSSESSION OF A FIREARM LAW
WAS DESIGNED FOR THE STREET IGNORANT;
HERE'S WHY

> Understanding isn't understanding until understanding is understood. Understand?
>
> *—Anonymous*

Six Arrested after Loaded Gun Dropped

Somewhere in the U.S. police arrested six men after they say one of them dropped a loaded revolver on the sidewalk when police approached them.

Police say the group of men was blocking the sidewalk in the 400 block of Ignorant Street, Friday night, causing people to walk into the street to go around them.

When the patrol officer intervened about 5:35 P.M., the men walked away as a member of the group dropped a loaded .357 caliber revolver on the ground.

Police arrested all the members of the group and each one was charged with felony possession of a firearm.

After reading this article that I clipped out of the newspaper, I said this would be a perfect example to explain to my readers what constructive possession is.

Constructive possession is when a firearm is in your reach or vicinity and the mental factor of you knowing that it's there. What do you mean? You are probably saying to yourself, what I mean is that you don't have to have a gun in your possession or on your person to be charged with the 922 (g). The gun can be in the residence that you stay in, it can be located in any room, it can be in the front yard by a tree, while you are sitting on the porch. It can be on top of the roof at a friend's house. It can be found in the doghouse in the backyard. While you are out front sitting in the car in the yard. That's what constructive possession is. The Feds feel if there is a gun anywhere around you and if it's not locked in a lockbox, then there is nothing stopping you from getting to it. The majority of firearm by a felon convictions came from this actual hypothesis.

A lot of offenders felt that they can or could beat this charge, because it first got thrown out by the State courts. But if the Feds picked the case up and are trying to get a conviction out of them, it's normally because they had an extensive criminal history and once the offender who felt that they could beat the charge sees how the Feds threw in some enhancements and probably superceded the indictment with other charges. Eventually the offender's mind changes, and he goes on ahead and try to get the best deal and plea out. Constructive possession is probably one of the most clever punitive strategies they have come up with to get convictions. Since the R.I.C.O. Act, which is short for Racketeer Influenced and Corrupt Organizations (Act), they use this act in some cases to incarcerate the entire neighborhood of street players that the Feds say were tied to illegal activity and conspiracies. This is one of the major defense schemes that the Feds use to incarcerate those that are street ignorant to this law.

In today's society people are packing and possessing guns everywhere. If you are a felon you have to come to the realization

Terry T. Ruffin

that you have to look after yourself and be careful how you move. All felons are not still engaging in illegal activity. You have a lot of felons that have wised up and have gotten out of the game and are moving forward doing constructive and productive things but that still does not exempt them from the firearm by felon or constructive possession law. I don't care how long you have been out of jail or have had a brush with the law. Let's not forget at the end of the day you are still a felon and if by chance you get pulled over and a firearm is in the car that belongs to a family member, to that police officer that weapon is yours. So let's not forget to check out your scenery and don't be afraid to ask questions that will save you a lot of trouble. Such as, do you have a gun anywhere in the house? Or is there a gun in this car? Your people may think you are trippin' but it's best for them to think that about you than for you to be hit with a Federal indictment for possession of firearm by felon and never say that a situation like the ones mentioned in this chapter can't happen to you. Every offender that I have ever met in the Federal prison that was doing time for constructive possession never thought that they could be charged with a gun that was not in their possession.

You see, once you are a felon and you have convictions on your criminal record. The Feds can take the convictions and turn them into a life sentence. I can't stipulate how important it is for you to take heed in all that I am saying. And it is a shame that offenders are doing lengthy bids and getting out and not sharing with their homies how the Feds railroaded them or put their backs against the wall and made them tap out with only hearsay evidence. Or somebody said that they had a gun doing an investigation was never caught with a gun when arrested, but was charged and convicted for one. These are the realities of the games that the Federal Government play with the lives of people that they feel are not valuable to anyone and they play these games of street chess with the street ignorant to keep the economy going and to monopolize off of the offenders, once they hit the yards of the Federal prisons. This is a very important chapter, don't forget all that was said and to be careful about your surroundings. There just may be a random or registered gun around your presence and if you are a felon. You can end up with a Federal prison sentence for something that you were not aware of.

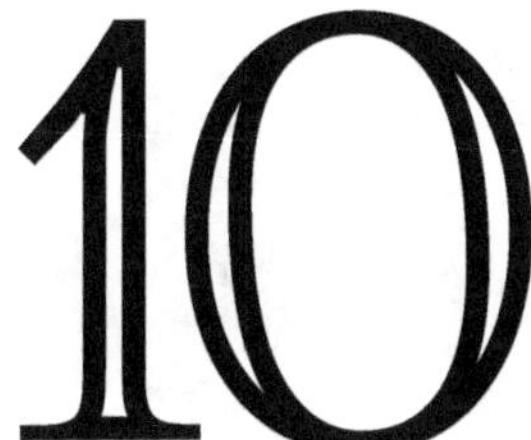

10

HOW FIREARM POSSESSION CAN RETIRE A FELON FROM THE STREETS DUE TO GUIDELINE ENHANCEMENTS: ALL YOU NEED IS OLD PRIORS

CHAPTER 10

HOW FIREARM POSSESSION CAN RETIRE A FELON FROM
THE STREETS DUE TO GUIDELINE ENHANCEMENTS:
ALL YOU NEED IS OLD PRIORS

> I tell all my students who become repeaters
> you're volunteering for slavery.
>
> —*Cindy Franz*

What more do I have to say about the importance of knowing gun laws and sharing with your peers and community, how detrimental it is for this awareness to be broadcasted in the streets of our communities where young men and women of color are jeopardizing their lives with elements of street life, guess what? There's even more. So far, we have covered a lot of valid information about gun possession, for the felon which can lead to a Federal indictment, constructive possession, which gives you a clear understanding of the fact that you don't even have to touch the gun if you are a felon. If the weapon is anywhere in your surroundings, you can be charged with a 922 (g) felony gun possession offence. Now I want to talk about Federal guideline enhancements, and what I consider to be a black eye for those that are still in the streets and especially for those that have retired their jerseys to the street life, and are now being an asset to their communities. If an offender has been arrested and convicted more than once for a felony, let's just say in particular a drug case, robbery, burglary or assault, then there is a 99% chance if he gets caught in possession of a firearm and is charged with a 922 (g) offense that he will also be enhanced by what is called the Arm Career Criminal Act of 1984, 18 U.S.C. 924 (e) (2) (B) (ii). Under this act a person who possesses a firearm after three or more convictions for a "serious drug offense" or a "violent felony" is subject to a minimum sentence of 15 years and a maximum sentence of life in prison 924(e) (1). So check this out, the max that you can get for the offense of firearm by felon is up to 10 years, but what the government has done is made it so that if a felon gets caught in possession of a gun and he has priors that consist of crimes of violence in the total of three, oh, and did I mention that the A.C.C.A. allows the Feds to use your criminal record, from whenever you first committed a crime, or got a conviction. Meaning if you pled guilty to a felony, when you were 12 years old, the Feds can use your juvenile record against you. You can receive a prison sentence (Federal) that is no less than 15 years, and if your criminal history is bad enough, you can get up to a life sentence. Yep, you can get 15 years to life for being in felony possession of a gun, because of your past criminal history.

The ACCA was established in 1984 and has been alive and well in the Federal Court system and has been utilized to incarcerate thousands of men of color every year throughout the United States. There have been a few cases that have disputed the A.C.C.A., such as the petitioner, Johnson v. United States, which stated that the A.C.C.A enhancement was unconstitutionally vague due to its residual clause. This case won in the Supreme Court because it shed light on the fact that a lot of people throughout the years were getting convicted on the strength of their past criminal history. And receiving a sentence of 15 years or more and their prior convictions weren't even considered to be crimes of violence. So the Johnson case came into effect

Terry T. Ruffin

June 2015. And has helped out a lot of offenders to either get time cuts or immediate releases. The fight is still on with other inmates who felt that their priors did not qualify them to receive such a harsh sentence that derived from the A.C.C.A. There are still numerous of Federal inmates trying to get relief from this enhancement clause, the Arm Career Criminal Act. The Supreme Court is bursting out of the seams with cases that oppose their convictions of A.C.C.A, saying that it should be void for vagueness. But at the same time since the Johnson case, or should I say in light of the Johnson, the Federal District Attorneys are doing everything they can to make sure that when they enhance an offender with the arm career criminal act. They are making sure that all i's are dotted and all t's are crossed. They are making sure that your past priors reflect the define acts of a "violent felony" as any crime punishable by imprisonment for a term exceeding one year… that—

> "(i) has an element the use, attempted use, or threatened use of physical force against the person of another: or

> "(ii) is burglary, arson, or extortion, involves use of explosives, or otherwise involves conduct that presents a serious potential risk of physical injury to another 924 (e) (2) (B)."

So if you are a street player and you are packing them pistols or riding dirty with someone who has one, always remember if you get pulled over that weapon belongs to you as well. And if you are a retired street player, got you a nine-to-five (job), going back to school, or just taking care of your family, then you too have to be careful about this 922 (g) offense along with the Arm Career

Criminal enhancement. The Feds don't care how long you have stayed out of the way and trouble or what kind of accomplishments you have made, or what kind of role model you have been to the youths in your community. If you got past criminal priors, even if the priors are twenty- to thirty-year-old priors, the Feds will use these priors against you. If you are caught in possession of a firearm or constructive possession of a firearm. Meaning you slipping and riding around with your girlfriends registered pistol and it's inside the glove compartment that's unlocked. Or inside of your bedroom that you both occupy in the closet or nightstand. If that pistol is not locked in a lockbox, if by any reason they have to search your home, when they find a gun, you're going to jail for constructive possession, no ifs, ands/or buts about it. The Feds will probably indict you. I'm in hopes that someone reading this book is getting the message loud and clear.

It is your responsibility to watch the company you keep and what's around you. You should make this a constant habit for you if you are a felon. You can't be ignorant to the criminal justice system games of entrapments. In this book I'm trying to make my language as plain as possible so that even a child can understand. So that there will be no excuse. And an awareness of how the Federal gun laws affect the people of color, living in impoverished or blue-collar communities, all over the United States of America.

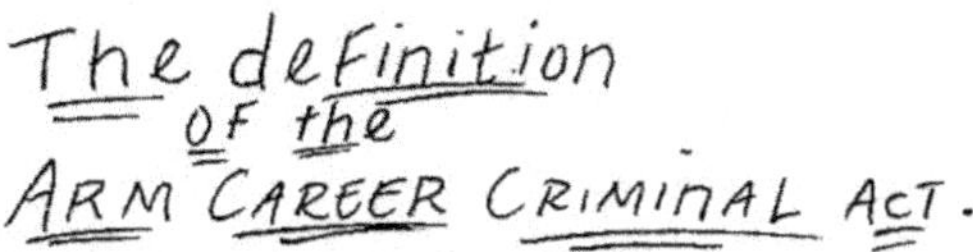

The Armed Career Criminal Act of 1984 (ACCA) is a U.S federal law that provides sentence enhancements for felons who commit crimes with firearms, if convicted of certain crimes three or more times. This law imposes special mandatory prison term of fifteen years on a felon who unlawfully possessed firearm, and has had three or more previous convictions for "violent felony" among others.

The Armed Career Criminal Act defines a "violent felony" as any crime punishable by imprisonment for a term exceeding one year that (i) has as an element the use, attempted use, or threatened use of physical force against the person of another; or (ii) is burglary, arson, or extortion, involves use of explosives, or otherwise involves conduct that presents a serious potential risk of physical injury to another. [18 U.S.C.S. § 924(e)(2)(B).]

The Armed Career Criminal Act focuses upon the special danger created when a particular type of offender like a violent criminal or drug trafficker who possesses a gun. In order to determine which offenders fall into this category, the Act looks to past crimes. This is because an offender's criminal history is relevant to the question whether s/he is a career criminal, or, more precisely, to the kind or degree of danger the offender would pose were he to possess a gun.

THE DEFINITION OF THE ARM CAREER CRIMINAL ACT

11

STREET PHILOSOPHY:
THE MUSIC AND THE VOICES AND
HOW IT'S DESTROYING OUR COMMUNITIES

CHAPTER 11

STREET PHILOSOPHY:
THE MUSIC AND THE VOICES AND HOW
IT'S DESTROYING OUR COMMUNITIES

> Conformity is the jailer of freedom and the enemy of growth.
>
> *—John F. Kennedy*

The common philosophy of the streets, is to be insensitive, to be loyal to your homies or those you rock with, and to get rich or die trying. These three schools of thought are exercised by the street players in the so-called game of the streets, in every predominantly African- and Latino-American hood all over the United States. It's these three factors that dictate the behavior and the mindset of those that partake in the illegal activities of the streets, and all of the tricks of the trade are passed on by words as well as deeds. The street player uses so much energy trying to accumulate money to keep up with the latest trend, of whatever it is that seems to bring satisfaction, that in course of doing so, they tend to lose themselves. The streets is a small world within a world and everything dealing with the street life allows each player to become somewhat selfish, watchful and distrustful. This type of aura has been imbedded and constantly promoted in our communities by the way of music that carries negative messages, and the voices of those that entertain those ignorant gestures.

For the street player, he has somewhat created his own atmosphere. He feels that the decisions he makes are accurate, the team he rolls with he feels are all solid and loyal, and in his mind, one day, he's gonna be on top of the world (rich) from the time that he has invested in doing his dirt. This way of thinking is only an illusion for those that partake in the wiles of the streets. For in a matter of time, that unhealthy, and unbalanced lifestyle will become such as a moth, that is tempted by a flame, self-destroyed from their own temptations of greed. This mentality of street ignorance is bred especially among young African-Americans and the lawless, careless, irresponsible, and self-consuming philosophy often leads the young street ignorant player, to committing murder of one of their own peers. Getting murdered by one of their peers, or receiving a life sentence, from partaking in some form of illegal activity. Today's hip-hop scene, is far from the intentions of building up our communities, as the early pioneers once envisioned as a voice, and tool to create awareness of self, our culture and to promote peace. We have more homicides in the African-American community a day, across the United States than the loss of American troops fighting terrorists in Syria a year. The numbers only seem to increase as time moves forward, and the motives for these killings are not even the usual common factor which is money. The true reasons why young African-Americans are getting gunned down in the streets is simply self-hate, and the ignorance of heritage and legacies. And I'm not talking about the legacies of street players of old that once terrorized the streets. I'm talking about the legacy of the people who fought for freedom, justice, and equality. The line of men and women of African-American heritage as well as some white Americans who fought through prayers, tears, bloodshed and loss of life for us to have the privileges like every other American has in this country today. There was once a time when the youth had respect for the

　　　　　Terry T. Ruffin

elders and parents of the communities, but the morality and the examples that are being set in some of the homes in urban neighborhoods are now coming from the music that paints the picture that gun toting, drug dealing and drug abuse is the epitome of the streets. And in order to be down, hip, or fit in, you must become insensitive, put your intellect on pause, and ride the wave of ignorance, bobbing your head to hooks and lyrics that create a bewildering mental atmosphere of hatred. That points the listeners right in the direction of violence or entangled in the criminal justice system, or becoming a statistic on black-on-black crime. This desensitized arena of thinking has become the philosophy of the streets, a psychological genocide that has young men of color dropping like flies to homicide related deaths and lengthy prison sentences, whether committed to State or Federal prison systems. This kind of philosophy has an overwhelming effect on the communities of the people of color, and also how the people who live on the outside of these communities, view the logic and violent tendencies of those who reside within these neighborhoods. Especially the people who work for public safety, such as the police.

Some authority figures, view every individual that exist in low-income-based environments as savages and inhuman. That's why when summoned or called for even the smallest incident for domestic disputes. The police are quick to act on their emotions of fear, and use deadly force on someone that may fear the authorities or police themselves, and don't know how to relate to the officials that he feels is out to get him. And it is this ignorance that is carried out by the residences that live in this fear, that cost them their lives for not complying with the verbal demands to keep their hands where the police can see them, and not make sudden moves when these trigger-happy officials are trying to ask questions or make an arrest. The Feds target these types of communities all over the

United States, they study the trends, the slang, listen to the lyrics of the music. They even hang out at all of the hotspots of all the street players such as the fancy nightclubs, pricey strip joints and the casinos. They know that the street players all patronize some of the same spots to either network or compete with one another, to see who's wearing what, doing what, and how much money they are spending. The most outlandish thing about all of this is, over 95% of this money that is so loosely being splurged, comes from out of the black community, from our own people whom are addicted to drugs and that spend whatever funds that come into the household to get high. And their habits support the street players' expensive night out. This type of activity is a good example of how our communities are drained from financial support and resources that would cause the hood to flourish economically but instead, it is being drained from our own ignorance. Another form of psychological assault that is putting a damper on our community is the voices that spread falsehood, fear and negative words that we use toward one another to tear down each other. And one word that is critical, that I will use for example, is the word nigga, which is now used mostly in all conversations among the street players. As a matter of fact, the word nigga is so freely used today, especially in the hip-hop culture, that I have even heard some white Americans use the word freely amongst some African-Americans and it caused no affect. Even in the Latino community they are addressing one another with the famous quote "What up, my nigga?" It is sad but it's true. This word is a slap in the face to the African-American but through ignorance, it has taken full reign in our communities and downplayed as ordinary street slang. But in reality, every time this word nigga is released in the air, it is as a wrecking ball. But instead of a building being demolished it's tearing down a group of people who fought hard for freedom, justice,

                    Terry T. Ruffin

and equality and the right to be addressed as human beings. Not the word nigga in which, the original use was a term that was used to belittle and annihilate the African descendant's character and wellbeing.

12

IF YOU'RE TAKING CHANCES, YOU
NEED TO MAKE FUNERAL ADVANCES

CHAPTER 12

IF YOU'RE TAKING CHANCES, YOU NEED TO MAKE FUNERAL ADVANCES

> Be not over much wicked neither be thou foolish, why should thou die before thy time?
>
> —*Ecclesiastes 7:17*

The rapid rising death toll in urban communities, especially African-Americans, has provoked alarm from pastors, local leaders, community members, and some concerned law enforcement. Every time we hear of somebody dying in the streets, the first thing that comes to the average person's mind is these two factors #1. I betcha the victim was a young black male and #2. I betcha he was shot or gunned down. It is a shame how a human life has no value among some of the young men of the African-American heritage. We have suffered attacks and murders from slavery, so-called freedom, all the way up to the Civil Rights Movement, where hundreds of black men and women lost their lives fighting for equality and respect for the African-American race. And even though our people have better conditions, through the Civil Rights Movement, somewhere down the line, we went from being hated by the same people who enslaved us, to hating ourselves. And this hate is highlighted in the African-American communities throughout the United States. Young black men are killing one another, like it's for sport and the motive is ignorance.

It's this ignorance that causes a man to shoot one of his peers, because he stays on the southside, and the southside and westside don't get along with one another. Or because a man is driving a better car than his, or this is a good one, check this out, he spoke to my girl real slick coming out of the store, so I'm going to kill him. These are some of the most dumbest excuses, for a man to go and take someone's life. That's why they call it senseless killings, because there is no real reason or excuse for these killings. The truth to this matter is, dealing with street ignorance there's a false sense of respect that each player feels he needs to have, and if violated he will go to every extreme to eliminate the one that committed the offense towards him. And in the process of his street ignorance he doesn't seem to care that he is eliminating himself as well, from his love ones and community. And as he sits in the county jail, he is filled with anguish and regrets, disattached from the streets that misled him and everyone that played a part of his life. Now living in a state of misery and all alone in realization that no one wants to have no parts of the life sentence, he is about to get.

But there is also two sides to every story, the same way that street ignorance can lead you to taking someone's life, it can also cause you to be a victim of homicide as well. When you are operating out of street ignorance running the streets, being lawless and careless, and involved in any and everything that can cause you consequences. You should at least have some respect for your loved ones by breaking them off some ends (money) out of your hard-earned bankroll, that you run the streets so hard for to help bury you. That's right, if you are taking chances in the streets with your life, you need to make funeral advances. This way the burden

     Terry T. Ruffin

of burying you will be taken care of and you would leave a legacy that at least you were selfish enough to leave money behind to bury your own remains.

The average funeral costs between 7,000 to 9,000 dollars. This includes viewing and burial, basic service fees, transporting your remains to the funeral home. A casket, embalming, and other preparations. The average cost of a funeral with cremation is 6,000 to 7,000 dollars, these costs do not include a cemetery, monument, marker, or other things like flowers. Many cemeteries require burial vaults or concrete grave box to ensure the ground will not give in over the casket, this vault also protects the remains from groundwater and insects activity. Everything that we do in life, comes with a price, and when you are putting yourself in positions, that your life can be taken at any time, due to your street ignorance then you need to make plans in advance, to pay your own funeral. I don't think that it is fair for someone, who is living riotous in the streets, to do something stupid, and get his life taken by an act of violence, and leave the burden on his family. This scenario happens every day in our communities. It's already hard enough to cope with the emotions of one dying, in some form of street violence, and to have that stigma to stay with them for the rest of their lives. As I was writing this chapter, I thought about not only do your homies, or so-called friends, abandon you when you catch a Fed case, they also abandon you, when your body is lying on that bed of steel in the city morgue. Those street partners won't even contribute anything toward your funeral. Some of them are even so lazy, they would not even commit to help carry your casket from the hearse to the inside of the church and back. This is something to think about. Who really has your back on the streets if something happens to you, and your life is taken? Remember the streets are predictable and when you are involving yourself around people who are selfish and street ignorant you shouldn't be in expectation for them to hold you or your family down, when a crisis or consequences hit. I hope that you are feeling me on this chapter, and take heed. But if you continue to persist on with your street ignorance, being desperate and always looking for gain from illegal means and feeling invincible. Be careful because sometimes, you will end up in a situation that you can't come back from. But if you want to disregard all that I have written in this chapter, then remember to at least not be selfish when it comes to giving your family some money to help bury you, when your time expires from your street ignorance.

COST BREAKDOWN OF FUNERAL SERVICES

The National Funeral Directors Association (NFDA) conducted a survey to calculate the median cost of a funeral. In 2018, the median cost was $7,360 without a vault: including the vault increase the cost to $8,755. This does not include the burial plot, headstone, flowers or an obituary.

Here is the funeral costs checklist included in the median funeral expenses in 2018, according to the NFDA:

Item	Cost
Funeral homes basic service fee (non-declinable)	$2,100
Transporting remains to funeral home	$325
Embalming	$725
Preparing the body in other ways, such as makeup and hairstyling	$250
Facilities and staff to manage a viewing	$425
Hearse	$325
Service car	$150
Basic memorial printed package	$160
Metal casket	$2400
Median cost of funeral with viewing and burial	$7360
Vault	$1395
Cost with fault	$8755

Many cemeteries require a burial vault or concrete grave box to ensure the ground will not buckle over the casket. A vault is reinforced to preserve the remains from groundwater and insect activity. When calculating funeral cost, you may have to include the cost of a vault or graveyard.

13

WHO IS TEACHING YOUR KIDS,
THE STREETS OR YOU?

CHAPTER 13

WHO IS TEACHING YOUR KIDS, THE STREETS OR YOU?

In today's society, it is kind of hard to keep up with all of the things that your child entertains, and if you're not a parent, then you may have nieces, nephews, younger siblings, or kids in your community that you help monitor and try to set good examples for. Street ignorance is always tapping at the door of every child's mind that are growing up in areas where illegal activity is running rampant. Normally the youths are influenced by what they see and hear, and if not monitored on a regular basis, no telling what they are being receptive and subjected to. One thing about kids is that they are curious and also easily misled.

You can tell your kids what to do and where to go, but if someone that is setting bad examples for them is spending more time with your child than you do, this could turn into a recipe for destruction. No, I'm not talking about other adults. I'm talking about other kids or peers that they may have befriended that you don't know who they are, where they live, and who their parents are and what type of parents they have. You see, your child may have befriended the neighborhood drug dealer's kid who has had no problem with exposing his child to the dangerous elements of street life. And in his child's eyes his father is a king and the Superman of his world. Can you blame him? He's a child, he doesn't know that is dad sells poison that is destroying lives and that he is putting his dearly beloved family in jeopardy. Question about this scenario, if the father who is a drug dealer is exposing his child to street ignorance, what is the drug dealer's son exposing your son or daughter to? We really have to be careful about who we let our children be around. Yeah, it's true, they are only kids, but the truth to this matter is that kids influence one another, and they also persuade each other in doing or saying things which is called peer pressure. And peer pressure can push a child into drug use, drug dealing, rape, murder and also suicide which is at an all-time high among the youths in the United States of America. Peer pressure can also cause their grades to fall and affect how they act in school, that's why it's so important to always check behind your child. Even concerning the music they listen to, or what they are watching on the television. Let's not forget a major factor that promotes street ignorance their computers, iPads, and cellphones. The culture of the streets, paints a carefree and lawless life through social media and a lot of the things that you see and hear are fictitious and the true facts will only manifest when your child copycats what they see and end up in a bad situation. Listen, don't be afraid to talk with your child about unprotected sex, drug use, drug dealing, guns, the value of human life, and how being street ignorant can put them in prison, or in a casket. Give it to them raw because if you don't somebody else may try to lead them in the wrong direction. If they taste the lies the streets have to offer, they just may like it and that good child that you thought you had, has now become street ignorant. We all are in this together each one teach one. Too many lives of African-

                    Terry T. Ruffin

and Latino-American young men are being lost to the streets through gun violence and incarcerations. It all starts in the home, there is nothing wrong with sitting your child down and telling them the truth about people, places, and things of the streets and how our people are destroying ourselves with senseless killings, drug abuse, and incarcerations. If you don't have your kids involved with positive activities such as sports, band, ROTC, Boys and Girls club, YMCA, community centers and other positive outlets, then this may be the time to start checking out the resources in your city, and if you got room take the neighbor's kid too, you'll be surprised how your mentorship will be an everlasting influence on their lives.

WHAT THE STREETS TEACH

A SPOKEN WORD POEM, WRITTEN BY THE AUTHOR:

A home is what you give
But the streets is where they live
You feed them so they grow
But the streets teach them what they know
You teach them how to have manners and show respect
The street teaches them disrespect and if violated put that fool
    in check
You teach them to honor thy mother and father
The street teaches them that parents don't know a thing
To listen to them: why bother?
You teach them to get good grades in school
To be somebody
To have a vision
The streets teach them how to say forget school
All I need is math to count my money
I can get my G.E.D. in prison
You teach your daughter how to be a good girl
Dress properly and keep her legs closed
The streets teaches her to wear skimpy clothes
And how to open her legs wide—
Now she's labeled a hoe
You teach your son how to be a man and take care
Of his responsibilities
The streets teach him how to be careless and wander
Around broke and responsibility free
You teach them about their history and to have a sense
Of black pride

Terry T. Ruffin

The streets teach them how to choose a flag
Without an option of dying before their time
You teach them how to be humble and how to keep
Their sanity
The streets teach them how to be violent
And to not have respect for humanity
You teach them to work hard and don't start nothing they
can't finish
The streets teach them how to put in work and
don't stop until they're dead or get a life sentence

My parents taught me everything I needed to know
But at the same time, the streets was teaching me too.
Just make sure that you spend more time with
Your kids than the streets
Because the streets to some, is a
Mother or Father too…

14

THE STREETS AND THE FEDS
BOTH WANT YOUR LIFE

CHAPTER 14

THE STREETS AND THE FEDS BOTH WANT YOUR LIFE

> Seems like every time you come up something happens to bring you back down.
>
> —*Tupac Shakur*

The streets and the Feds have one thing in common: they both want your life. Statistics show, that in the game of the streets, it is almost the same percentage between street players that are getting killed from street violence and the street players that are getting indicted, convicted, and receiving life sentences. It struck me one day as I was reading some legal service reports there was a certain brief that stood out to me. In this article the reporter was interviewing a Federal inmate who had just been released from Federal prison a year ago, and was back in Federal custody on new charges facing a life sentence. When the reporter asked him what was his regrets? He stated that he only wished that he died in the streets like the rest of his homies than to be in Federal prison for the rest of his life. To me this was not an understatement, because when I was doing a Federal bid, I met plenty of comrades that felt the same way and wished that they would have died in the streets. Street life is so alluring, that to some of the street players, they are committed even unto the death. Pledging the allegiance to a philosophy, that only allows the player to be watchful of two different consequences that craps them out from the streets physically, or eternally. You see, when you are operating out of street ignorance, the entire mission of this philosophy is to kill your true potential. That would allow you to fulfill your God-given purpose, everybody has one. The streets only suck that potential out of you, or puts you in a position that you can't live it out, due to the hinderances of street life. Believe it or not, the Federal prison system does the same thing. You may still be alive while you are doing your sentence, but your true purpose is also being unfulfilled, because you can't contribute anything to your family, friends, or society.

The Feds take criminal conduct very seriously, it's their game, their rules and complex system that affects your life when you become entangled in their mindboggling world. The same as the streets which has a complicated system as well, with rules and codes that the street players often break, when true reality hits the surface of the street ignorant mind. And both of these systems is a threat to young African- and Latino-Americans who fall victim to the wiles of the streets, and end up in the Federal prison system or a coffin. The streets and the Feds both want your life, to terminate your existence, and to turn your life into a statistic. These two systems the streets, and the Feds affect our communities drastically taking a vast number of men and women who just thought they were trying to survive in a world that has counted them out. Because they didn't have their high school diploma, or G.E.D., or because they were a convicted felon, or just because they never knew how to make healthy choices, due to growing up in an unhealthy environment. Our communities have always been unaware of the true distractions of the streets, and the Federal prison system. And how it has become a warehouse to house human beings, mostly African- and Latino-Americans. Or how six out of every 10 young men, will die from some form of street violence right in their own community.

     Terry T. Ruffin

More than two million people are incarcerated in the United States, more than any other country in the world. And tens of billions of taxpayers' dollars are spent annually to keep them there. So if billions of taxpayers' funds are used to house inmates, in prisons all over the United States then, where is the funds for prison reform, more halfway houses, drug programs, and reentry agencies? The Feds spend more money to house prisoners than to rehabilitate or reform them. Without these entities the released prisoner does not stand a chance successfully reentering their communities. They come out of prison to only fall back into the street ignorance that got them there. It's a cycle and for those that are on this merry-go-round, it's hard to get off of and it's crazy because neither the Feds who are watching, or the streets that's trying to put you there, don't give a damn about you, they both just want your life.

They both want you to be street ignorant, to sacrifice your life, for their system that is made to destroy you, mentally and physically. And the Feds will let you play in the streets, because they know sooner or later that if the streets don't kill you, their sentence guideline will. This is not a myth and it may not be televised, but we have the street players getting killed or snatched up by the Feds every day throughout the United States. Why is it, that no one is noticing these facts? Why don't the hundreds of Federal prisoners that get released from prison, get out and not bring awareness to the communities? The truth really is that, the Feds and the streets are their greatest enemy, and they both are trying to kill them. And these two bad boys have always moved in silence. Think about it.

15

DON'T BE IGNORANT;
EDUCATE YOURSELF ABOUT THE LAWS
OF THE LAND AND YOUR
CONSTITUTIONAL RIGHTS

CHAPTER 15

DON'T BE IGNORANT;
EDUCATE YOURSELF ABOUT THE LAWS OF THE LAND
AND YOUR CONSTITUTIONAL RIGHTS

The roots of education are bitter, but the fruit is sweet.

—Aristotle

In this book, we have covered so many facts and damaging consequences pertaining to the realities of street life and the street ignorance that causes us to move unconsciously on a quest to self-destruction. I have attempted to paint a picture bursting with colors of knowledge and awareness of things that would cause affliction to you if you are ignorant of the wiles of the street. I can't even begin to put in words how important it is for you to stay aware to the things in your environment that will eventually cause you and your family grief or mourning. The street life is a one-way direction and headed on a destination called nowhere. You may try to find shortcuts as you travel this road but whether you get to nowhere fast or slow, it's still nowhere. In order for you not to be a victim of street ignorance you must educate yourself on things that you feel are not important, or the things you feel don't apply to you. Remember what I said in the introduction of this book, that it's the things that you don't know that will hurt you. Knowing the laws of the land can save you and if every law that is written applies to you, that means in some form of fashion they can affect you. The state as well as Federal Court rooms are filled up with cases from offenders who have the slightest idea of what is going on. As their lawyers (public defenders) represent them bargaining deals with the District Attorney that will take them off of the streets for a few years or for the rest of their lives. Some offenders catch bids and don't even know what they pleaded out to, or the minimum or maximum sentence that the charge actually carries. This is one of the craziest things I have seen dealing with a street-ignorant offender. How do you plead guilty to something or a charge that you don't even know how much time it carries? Why would you plea to anything first without knowing if your constitutional rights have been violated? The criminal justice system uses this theory to their advantage because they know if you are ignorant to the law or of the law, then they can basically do anything to you. And they will continue to arrest you, indict you, and convict you for anything until you learn about your constitutional rights and what the authorities can and cannot do. Every game has rules and if you are playing their game and not know the rules, you will lose every single time. You notice that I said their game, because when you're involved into illegal activity and you have no awareness of the hidden consequences then you're playing their game, they know more about you than you know yourself. And it is easy for them when they know that their opponent doesn't know how to strategize and play the game.

Knowing your constitutional rights allow you to know the difference between abiding by the law or when your rights are being violated. The street player can be one of the best chess players in the world. He can know all of the right moves to defend his chess opponent on the chess game board, but he can't defend himself for even the simplest traffic tickets. I'm not telling you to go and learn

     Terry T. Ruffin

your constitutional rights to commit a crime in hopes of what you learned will help you defend yourself. No, I'm telling you that by you knowing your rights, this will not only help you in a sense with your legal issues, it will also help you with your civil issues such as your right to vote, your freedom of speech, your right to exercise your religion. And a very important amendment among the street player, is an illegal search and seizures which is the IV amendment that states that the right of the people to be secure in their persons, houses, papers, and effects against unreasonable searches and seizures, shall not be violated, and no warrants shall issue, but upon probable cause, supported by oath or affirmation, and particularly describing the place to be searched, and the persons or things to be seized.

This amendment has been a key to freedom to thousands of state and Federal inmates who studied their case and seen where they were violated in a court of law. And this knowledge allowed them to file motions that eventually made the courts release them. In courtrooms all over the United States they are illegally incarcerating thousands of African- as well as Latino-Americans a day, due to plea bargains and found guilty trial verdicts that were oppressed upon the street ignorant or those that did not have an understanding of the law. When you are about running the streets catching all sorts of frivolous cases, not only will this affect your criminal record, but anytime you catch a case they will always use your past criminal history against you. Believe me, this will lead up to you doing a lot of prison time in the long run. I will say this again, street life has no wins and will only help you lose your place in society or dig yourself an early grave. There will be some who read this book that will disregard all that they have read and continue on to destroy their lives from street ignorance. If that is your intention, then at least learn the laws and what affects you, that way the D.A.

just can't do anything with you in the court that you already are not aware of. But if you are one of the ones that are going to take heed, and educate yourself to laws, that are freely given for your edification. This will be a good look toward your future and also knowledge and power to any element of the law, when you're faced with it. The Constitution of the Bill of Rights are for every citizen of the United States. These amendments are what govern and regulate the court of law and these bills are very important for the African- and Latino-Americans that stay not only in impoverished communities, but in middle- and high-class communities as well. I've mentioned not only the poor people of color, but for the rich people of color as well because they also fall into the same category, as any other colored American when it comes to the civil or criminal justice system. The reason so is because, racism is still alive and well in America and some authority figures still use racism as the motivation to harass, antagonize and even kill men and women of color, who they may see or feel that they are a threat to their well-being. If the wealthy people of color that are conscious to these Bill of Rights that govern the land still have a hard time seeking equality, the street ignorant across the country who reside in urban impoverished communities have no chance, period! Therefore, the street player must educate themselves on their civil as well as human rights, to know if they have been violated or not.

If we as a community promoted this awareness in some of our daily conversations to young men and women of color who are at risk to the casualties of the streets, not only will you be opening someone's eyes to the big picture of these realities, but you will also be detouring them from future consequences of street ignorance. Each one, teach one. This old African proverb put in action can save someone's life. On the next page you will find the beginning page of the full copy of the Bill of Rights. If you were born in

 Terry T. Ruffin

the United States of America, these rights apply to you! Study them and make copies and pass the materials along to other street players in the community.

Amendments

The Bill of Rights

Preamble

THE Conventions of a number of the States having at the time of their adopting the Constitution, expressed a desire, in order to prevent misconstruction or abuse of its powers, that further declaratory and restrictive clauses should be added: And as extending the ground of public confidence in the Government, will best insure the beneficent ends of its institution

Amendment I

Congress shall make no law respecting an establishment of religion, or prohibiting the free exercise thereof; or abridging the freedom of speech, or of the press; or the right of the people peaceably to assemble, and to petition the Government for a redress of grievances.

Amendment II

A well regulated Militia, being necessary to the security of a free State, the right of the people to keep and bear Arms, shall not be infringed.

Amendment III

No Soldier shall, in time of peace be quartered in any house, without the consent of the Owner, nor in time of war, but in a manner to be prescribed by law.

Amendment IV

The right of the people to be secure in their persons, houses, papers, and effects, against unreasonable searches and seizures, shall not be violated, and no Warrants shall issue, but upon probable cause, supported by Oath or affirmation, and particularly describing the place to be searched, and the persons or things to be seized.

Amendment V

No person shall be held to answer for a capital, or otherwise infamous crime, unless on a presentment or indictment of a Grand Jury, except in cases arising in the land or naval forces, or in the Militia, when in actual service in time of War or public danger; nor shall any person be subject for the same offence to be twice put in jeopardy of life or limb; nor shall be compelled in any criminal case to be a witness against himself, nor be deprived of life, liberty, or property, without due process of law; nor shall private property be taken for public use, without just compensation.

Amendment VI

In all criminal prosecutions, the accused shall enjoy the right to a speedy and public trial, by an impartial jury of the State and district wherein the crime shall have been committed, which district shall have been previously ascertained by law, and to be informed of the nature and cause of the accusation; to be confronted with the witnesses against him; to have compulsory process for obtaining witnesses in his favor, and to have the Assistance of Counsel for his defence.

Terry T. Ruffin

Amendment VII

In Suits at common law, where the value in controversy shall exceed twenty dollars, the right of trial by jury shall be preserved, and no fact tried by a jury, shall be otherwise re-examined in any Court of the United States, than according to the rules of the common law.

Amendment VIII

Excessive bail shall not be required, nor excessive fines imposed, nor cruel and unusual punishments inflicted.

Amendment IX

The enumeration in the Constitution, of certain rights, shall not be construed to deny or disparage others retained by the people.

Amendment X

The powers not delegated to the United States by the Constitution, nor prohibited by it to the States, are reserved to the States respectively, or to the people.

Additional Amendments

Amendment XI

The Judicial power of the United States shall not be construed to extend to any suit in law or equity, commenced or prosecuted against one of the United States by Citizens of another State, or by Citizens or Subjects of any Foreign State.

Amendment XII

The Electors shall meet in their respective states and vote by ballot for President and Vice-President, one of whom, at least, shall not be an inhabitant of the same state with themselves; they shall name in their ballots the person voted for as President, and in distinct ballots the person voted for as Vice-President, and they shall make distinct lists of all persons voted for as President, and of all persons voted for as Vice-President, and of the number of votes for each, which lists they shall sign and certify, and transmit sealed to the seat of the government of the United States, directed to the President of the Senate;-The President of the Senate shall, in the presence of the Senate and House of Representatives, open all the certificates and the votes shall then be counted;-The person having the greatest Number of votes for President, shall be the President, if such number be a majority of the whole number of Electors appointed; and if no person have such majority, then from the persons having the highest numbers not exceeding three on the list of those voted for as President, the House of Representatives shall choose immediately, by ballot, the President. But in choosing the President, the votes shall be taken by states, the representation from each state having one vote; a quorum for this purpose shall consist of a member or members from two-thirds of the states, and a majority of all the states shall be necessary to a choice. And if the House of Representatives shall not choose a President whenever the right of choice shall devolve upon them, before the fourth day of March next following, then the Vice-President shall act as President, as in the case of the death or other constitutional disability of the President-The person having the greatest number of votes as VicePresident, shall be the Vice-President, if such number be a majority of the whole number of Electors appointed, and if no person have a majority, then from the two highest numbers on the list, the Senate shall choose the Vice-President; a quorum for the purpose shall consist of two-thirds of the whole number of Senators, and a majority of the whole number shall be necessary to a choice. But no person constitutionally ineligible to the office of President shall be eligible to that of Vice-President of the United States.

Amendment XIII

Section 1

Neither slavery nor involuntary servitude, except as a punishment for crime whereof the party shall have been duly convicted, shall exist within the United States, or any place subject to their jurisdiction.

Section 2

Congress shall have power to enforce this article by appropriate legislation.

Amendment XIV

Section 1

All persons born or naturalized in the United States and subject to the jurisdiction thereof, are citizens of the United States and of the State wherein they reside. No State shall make or enforce any law which shall abridge the privileges or immunities of citizens of the United States; nor shall any State deprive any person of life, liberty, or property, without due process of law; nor deny to any person within its jurisdiction the equal protection of the laws.

Terry T. Ruffin

Section 2

Representatives shall be apportioned among the several States according to their respective numbers, counting the whole number of persons in each State, excluding Indians not taxed. But when the right to vote at any election for the choice of electors for President and Vice President of the United States, Representatives in Congress, the Executive and Judicial officers of a State, or the members of the Legislature thereof, is denied to any of the male inhabitants of such State, being twenty-one years of age, and citizens of the United States, or in any way abridged, except for participation in rebellion, or other crime, the basis of representation therein shall be reduced in the proportion which the number of such male citizens shall bear to the whole number of male citizens twenty-one years of age in such State.

Section 3

No person shall be a Senator or Representative in Congress, or elector of President and Vice President, or hold any office, civil or military, under the United States, or under any State, who, having previously taken an oath, as a member of Congress, or as an officer of the United States, or as a member of any State legislature, or as an executive or judicial officer of any State, to support the Constitution of the United States, shall have engaged in insurrection or rebellion against the same, or given aid or comfort to the enemies thereof. But Congress may by a vote of two-thirds of each House, remove such disability.

Section 4

The validity of the public debt of the United States, authorized by law, including debts incurred for payment of pensions and bounties for services in suppressing insurrection or rebellion, shall not be questioned. But neither the United States nor any State shall assume or pay any debt or obligation incurred in aid of insurrection or rebellion against the United States, or any claim for the loss or emancipation of any slave; but all such debts, obligations and claims shall be held illegal and void.

Section 5

The Congress shall have power to enforce, by appropriate legislation, the provisions of this article.

Amendment XV

Section 1

The right of citizens of the United States to vote shall not be denied or abridged by the United States or by any State on account of race, color, or previous condition of servitude.

Section 2

The Congress shall have power to enforce this article by appropriate legislation.

Amendment XVI

The Congress shall have power to lay and collect taxes on incomes, from whatever source derived, without apportionment among the several States, and without regard to any census or enumeration.

Amendment XVII

The Senate of the United States shall be composed of two Senators from each State, elected by the people thereof, for six years; and each Senator shall have one vote. The electors in each State shall have the qualifications requisite for electors of the most numerous branch of the State legislatures.

When vacancies happen in the representation of any State in the Senate, the executive authority of such State shall issue writs of election to fill such vacancies: Provided, That the legislature of any State may empower the executive thereof to make temporary appointments until the people fill the vacancies by election as the legislature may direct.

This amendment shall not be so construed as to affect the election or term of any Senator chosen before it becomes valid as part of the Constitution.

Amendment XVIII

Section 1

After one year from the ratification of this article the manufacture, sale, or transportation of intoxicating liquors within, the importation thereof into, or the exportation thereof from the United States and all territory subject to the jurisdiction thereof for beverage purposes is hereby prohibited.

Section 2

The Congress and the several States shall have concurrent power to enforce this article by appropriate legislation.

Section 3

This article shall be inoperative unless it shall have been ratified as an amendment to the Constitution by the legislatures of the several States, as provided in the Constitution, within seven years from the date of the submission hereof to the States by the Congress.

Amendment XIX

The right of citizens of the United States to vote shall not be denied or abridged by the United States or by any State on account of sex.

Congress shall have power to enforce this article by appropriate legislation.

     Terry T. Ruffin

Amendment XX

Section 1

The terms of the President and Vice President shall end at noon on the 20th day of January, and the terms of Senators and Representatives at noon on the 3d day of January, of the years in which such terms would have ended if this article had not been ratified; and the terms of their successors shall then begin.

Section 2

The Congress shall assemble at least once in every year, and such meeting shall begin at noon on the 3d day of January, unless they shall by law appoint a different day.

Section 3

If, at the time fixed for the beginning of the term of the President, the President elect shall have died, the Vice President elect shall become President. If a President shall not have been chosen before the time fixed for the beginning of his term, or if the President elect shall have failed to qualify, then the Vice President elect shall act as President until a President shall have qualified; and the Congress may by law provide for the case wherein neither a President elect nor a Vice President elect shall have qualified, declaring who shall then act as President, or the manner in which one who is to act shall be selected, and such person shall act accordingly until a President or Vice President shall have qualified.

Section 4

The Congress may by law provide for the case of the death of any of the persons from whom the House of Representatives may choose a President whenever the right of choice shall have devolved upon them, and for the case of the death of any of the persons from whom the Senate may choose a Vice President whenever the right of choice shall have devolved upon them.

Section 5

Sections 1 and 2 shall take effect on the 15th day of October following the ratification of this article.

Section 6

This article shall be inoperative unless it shall have been ratified as an amendment to the Constitution by the legislatures of three-fourths of the several States within seven years from the date of its submission.

Amendment XXI

Section 1

The eighteenth article of amendment to the Constitution of the United States is hereby repealed.

Section 2

The transportation or importation into any State, Territory, or possession of the United States for delivery or use therein of intoxicating liquors, in violation of the laws thereof, is hereby prohibited.

Section 3

This article shall be inoperative unless it shall have been ratified as an amendment to the Constitution by conventions in the several States, as provided in the Constitution, within seven years from the date of the submission hereof to the States by the Congress.

Amendment XXII

Section 1

No person shall be elected to the office of the President more than twice, and no person who has held the office of President, or acted as President, for more than two years of a term to which some other person was elected President shall be elected to the office of the President more than once. But this Article shall not apply to any person holding the office of President, when this Article was proposed by the Congress, and shall not prevent any person who may be holding the office of President, or acting as President, during the term within which this Article becomes operative from holding the office of President or acting as President during the remainder of such term.

Section 2

This article shall be inoperative unless it shall have been ratified as an amendment to the Constitution by the legislatures of three-fourths of the several States within seven years from the date of its submission to the States by the Congress.

Amendment XXIII

Section 1

The District constituting the seat of Government of the United States shall appoint in such manner as the Congress may direct:

A number of electors of President and Vice President equal to the whole number of Senators and Representatives in Congress to which the District would be entitled if it were a State, but in no event more than the least populous State; they shall be in addition to those appointed by the States, but they shall be considered, for the purposes of the election of President and Vice President, to be electors appointed by a State; and they shall meet in the District and perform such duties as provided by the twelfth article of amendment.

Section 2

The Congress shall have power to enforce this article by appropriate legislation.

Amendment XXIV

Section 1

The right of citizens of the United States to vote in any primary or other election for President or Vice President for electors for President or Vice President, or for Senator or Representative in Congress, shall not be denied or abridged by the United States or any State by reason of failure to pay any poll tax or other tax.

Section 2

The Congress shall have power to enforce this article by appropriate legislation.

Amendment XXV

Section 1

In case of the removal of the President from office or of his death or resignation, the Vice President shall become President.

Section 2

Whenever there is a vacancy in the office of the Vice President, the President shall nominate a Vice President who shall take office upon confirmation by a majority vote of both Houses of Congress.

Section 3

Whenever the President transmits to the President pro tempore of the Senate and the Speaker of the House of Representatives his written declaration that he is unable to discharge the powers and duties of his office, and until he transmits to them a written declaration to the contrary, such powers and duties shall be discharged by the Vice President as Acting President.

Section 4

Whenever the Vice President and a majority of either the principal officers of the executive departments or of such other body as Congress may by law provide, transmit to the President pro tempore of the Senate and the Speaker of the House of Representatives their written declaration that the President is unable to discharge the powers and duties of his office, the Vice President shall immediately assume the powers and duties of the office as Acting President.

Thereafter, when the President transmits to the President pro tempore of the Senate and the Speaker of the House of Representatives his written declaration that no inability exists, he shall resume the powers and duties of his office unless the Vice President and a majority of either the principal officers of the executive department or of such other body as Congress may by law provide, transmit within four days to the President pro tempore of the Senate and the Speaker of the House of Representatives their written declaration that the President is unable to discharge the powers and duties of his office. Thereupon Congress shall decide the issue, assembling within forty-eight hours for that purpose if not in session. If the Congress, within twenty-one days after receipt of the latter written declaration, or, if Congress is not in session, within twenty-one days after Congress is required to assemble, determines by two-thirds vote of both Houses that the President is unable to discharge the powers and duties of his office, the Vice President shall continue to discharge the same as Acting President; otherwise, the President shall resume the powers and duties of his office.

Amendment XXVI

Section 1

The right of citizens of the United States, who are eighteen years of age or older, to vote shall not be denied or abridged by the United States or by any State on account of age.

Section 2

The Congress shall have power to enforce this article by appropriate legislation.

Amendment XXVII

No law varying the compensation for the services of the Senators and Representatives shall take effect, until an election of Representatives shall have intervened.

 Terry T. Ruffin

16

FELONS MATTER IN THE STREETS;
LET'S MAKE A DIFFERENCE

CHAPTER 16

FELONS MATTER IN THE STREETS; LET'S MAKE A DIFFERENCE

> It's not too late to be what you might have been.
>
> —*Anonymous*

When some people hear the word felon, a negative image of some sort crosses their mind. Throughout history of the United States, the word felon has always been related to, as the bad guy. One who breaks the laws, go to prison, get released and breaks the law all over again. To the criminal justice system, the felon is a product, to society an outcast, and to the felon, it's a stigma that their stained with for the rest of their lives. Being a felon to some is an excuse to continue the behavior of a felon, careless, irresponsible and lawless. But all felons don't view this incriminating label as an excuse to give up and throw in the towel. There are a lot of felons who have once upon a time, made some bad choices, got arrested, put on probation, or did a prison sentence and was released and moved on to be a contribution to their communities, as well as humanity.

We all make mistakes in life, some are greater than others, but the key to this factor is, just because you have fallen, does not mean that you have to stay there. There is no greater encouragement than for someone to see an individual, who was once at the bottom, whether from a crisis, circumstance, or consequence, took their bad situation as a stepping stone and rose back to the top. Felons all over the United States, are doing just that. In today's society making a difference and reaching for the stars. I have even met some felons with better-paying jobs than non-felons, and that is why felons, or those that have been convicted of a crime, whether past or present, have no excuse! We are no longer counted out, and we have just as much of a right to be successful as anyone else. If you are a felon, and are now reading these words, I wanna say to you, that you can make a difference! You may not think that what you went through while incarcerated, meant anything but let me tell you my brothers, or sisters, that it means a lot, and your story can help change somebody's life! Think of it this way, you have people that are being effective to the communities, and they haven't even been through the struggle. Imagine how your story can affect someone that is now walking in the shoes that you once worn.

It's time for felons to have a voice, it's time for felons to share with the world their experiences. Whether it was past drug addictions, drug dealing, robbing, stealing or just being plain out street ignorant. Your voice needs to be heard. And for the felons who just sometimes feel like giving up, because of the stigma of being a felon. Or can't seem to get a job, or you are just having a hard time trying to do the right thing and adjust to society, don't give up! You still have a chance, and most important you are FREE! Free to make good choices, and stay free. You no longer have anyone telling you when to go to bed, and when to get up, when you can use the phone, or go to Rec. Or just telling you what to do period. Even if you are on probation, you are still free, to move about as you please, and you now have the opportunity to connect with re-

                    Terry T. Ruffin

sources and people that will be safety nets for you, as you strive to do the right thing. You can too, be a productive and successful citizen in this society. The Federal Government wants Americans to feel that people who have felons on their criminal record can't be trusted, and eventually will commit crimes, that will put them back in prison again. This ideology, only gives them the excuse to drain the American taxpayers, for funding to build more prisons, and so-called programs with the blind concept to reduce recidivism rates. But from my research while putting together this book, I've noticed that the media, will highlight a felon that just got out of prison, committing another crime and going back inside the institution. But rarely would you hear the media speak about the felon who made a mistake, paid their debt, and was released to go out into society and make a difference by giving back to his community. And gone from being a reject to an asset to humanity.

It is too many men and women of color, who are felons that are still street ignorant and doing the same thing over and over again, and expecting different results. That's called insanity. For the felons who have been to prison more than once. Your family, and some of your friends, that live law-abiding lives think that you are really insane. To be going back and forth in such a mindboggling place (prison). But what they don't know is really it's not because the police are always harassing you. And accusing you of something to send you back to prison. The truth is, it is because of your choices and street ignorance that puts you back where you really wanted to be. You may be saying to yourself, what does the brother mean by what he just said? Let me tell you what I mean. The reality is that when you are playing in the streets committing crimes, getting high, being disrespectful to your family and abandoning your kids. When the prison door slams behind you. You and only you know, that you did it to yourself. This don't have to be your scenario anymore. Let's as felons no longer look back in the past and moved forward by educating ourselves, teaching others what we have learned through our experiences, and making a difference in a society, that once counted us out! The sky is the limit! And you can be anything that you want to be in this life, if you put your mind to it. If you have just completed this book, <u>let's make a difference</u>!!! Street ignorance to you now is only an excuse.

A SMALL PRAYER FOR THE FELON

<u>Oh God, I thank you that my life is not in vain.</u>

Amen.

            Terry T. Ruffin

APPENDICES

APPENDIX 1

JOURNAL EXERCISE

In the space provided, write down your personal thoughts about each chapter. For each chapter ask the following questions.

1. What did I learn about street ignorance?

2. How important is this information?

3. How has street ignorance affected me?

4. What will I do in response to what I learned?

Chapter 1:   People, Places, and Things of the Streets

____

____

____

____

____

____

____

Chapter 2:   Street Sense Sometimes Makes No Sense

Chapter 3:   The Streets (Predictable or Unpredictable?)

                    Terry T. Ruffin

Chapter 5:   Street Hustling and Addictions

Chapter 6:   The Prosperity and Poverty of the Streets

____

____

____

____

____

____

____

Chapter 7:   Priors and Convictions Your Street Credibility,
              It All Adds Up

____

____

____

____

____

____

                    Terry T. Ruffin

Chapter 8:	Guns and Federal Guidelines Give an Ignorant
		Felon a Lot of Time

Chapter 9:	The Constructive Possession of a Firearm Law Was
		Designed for the Street Ignorant; Here's Why

Terry T. Ruffin

Chapter 12:   If You're Taking Chances, You Need to Make
Funeral Advances

____

____

____

____

____

____

Chapter 13:   Who Is Teaching Your Kids, the Streets or You?

____

____

____

____

____

____

____

Chapter 14:   The Streets and the Feds Both Want Your Life

____

____

____

____

____

____

Chapter 15:   Don't Be Ignorant; Educate Yourself about the
               Laws of the Land and Your Constitutional Rights

____

____

____

____

____

____

____

                    Terry T. Ruffin

____

____

____

____

____

____

____

____

APPENDIX 2

DID-YOU-KNOW FACTS CONCERNING FEDERAL LAWS

Did you know that?

#1 If you get arrested for a firearm anywhere within a 1000 feet from a school or college, and if you have the credentials of being a felon, you qualify for a Federal indictment and you can be sentenced up under a mandatory minimum sentence, and that minimum maybe 20 years if you got priors.

The term "school zone" means:

(A) in, or on the grounds of, a public, parochial or private school; or

(B) within a distance of 1000 feet from the grounds of a public, parochial, or private school

#2 Did you know that?

Any person that is arrested for distributing, possessing with intent to distribute, or manufacturing a controlled substance in or on, or within the thousand (1000 feet) of real property compromising a public or private elementary, vocational, or secondary school or a public or private college, a junior college, or university, or a playground, or housing facility owned by a public housing authority, or within 100 feet of a public or private youth center, public swimming, or video arcade facility is subject to twice the maximum punishment. The Feds will eat this up in front of a jury of 12 and will paint a picture of you as the scum of the earth. Being street ignorant of this violation will cost you in the long run.

Trust me, you'll be better off putting in job applications, what do you have to lose? Besides, you just may get the job!

#3 DID YOU KNOW THAT?

If you are a felon, you can be indicted for the 922(g) firearm by felon offense for being in possession of an antique firearm. All it needs to have is a matchlock, flintlock, percussion cap, or similar type of ignition system manufactured in or before 1898. And as a felon you qualify for a federal indictment and you can be sentenced under the 0-to-120-month federal guidelines. So, if you have one, it may look old as dust and it may not even shoot but if it has a firing pin, it's 922(g) material for a felon.

#4 DID YOU KNOW THAT?

A defendant who has been found guilty of an offense may be sentenced to a term of imprisonment.

The authorized terms for the United States of America are as follows:

1. For a Class-A felony, not more than twenty-five years
2. For a Class-B felony, no more than twelve years
3. For a Class-C felony, no more than twelve years
4. For a Class-D felony, not more than six years
5. For a Class-E felony, not more than three years
6. For a Class Misdemeanor, not more than one year

7. For a Class Misdemeanor, not more than six months

8. For a Class-C misdemeanor, not more than 30 days; and

9. fourth infraction, not more than five days

So if you are not a felon, stick to the infraction category.

#5 Did you know that?

If you graduate from the state courtroom to the Federal System you're no longer dealing with felony class authorized terms of imprisonment. The Feds have their own way of doing things. All sentences are calculated by the offense level and your criminal history (priors). The more priors you have the more time you will be looking at. Can't forget the unknown enhancements that they somehow throw in. Check out the sentencing table.

SENTENCING TABLE
(in months of imprisonment)

	Offense Level	Criminal History Category (Criminal History Points)					
		I (0 or 1)	II (2 or 3)	III (4, 5, 6)	IV (7, 8, 9)	V (10, 11, 12)	VI (13 or more)
Zone A	1	0-6	0-6	0-6	0-6	0-6	0-6
	2	0-6	0-6	0-6	0-6	0-6	1-7
	3	0-6	0-6	0-6	0-6	2-8	3-9
	4	0-6	0-6	0-6	2-8	4-10	6-12
	5	0-6	0-6	1-7	4-10	6-12	9-15
	6	0-6	1-7	2-8	6-12	9-15	12-18
Zone B	7	0-6	2-8	4-10	8-14	12-18	15-21
	8	0-6	4-10	6-12	10-16	15-21	18-24
	9	4-10	6-12	8-14	12-18	18-24	21-27
Zone C	10	6-12	8-14	10-16	15-21	21-27	24-30
	11	8-14	10-16	12-18	18-24	24-30	27-33
	12	10-16	12-18	15-21	21-27	27-33	30-37
	13	12-18	15-21	18-24	24-30	30-37	33-41
	14	15-21	18-24	21-27	27-33	33-41	37-46
	15	18-24	21-27	24-30	30-37	37-46	41-51
	16	21-27	24-30	27-33	33-41	41-51	46-57
	17	24-30	27-33	30-37	37-46	46-57	51-63
	18	27-33	30-37	33-41	41-51	51-63	57-71
	19	30-37	33-41	37-46	46-57	57-71	63-78
	20	33-41	37-46	41-51	51-63	63-78	70-87
	21	37-46	41-51	46-57	57-71	70-87	77-96

22	41-51	46-57	51-63	63-78	77-96	84-105
23	46-57	51-63	57-71	70-87	84-105	92-115
24	51-63	57-71	63-78	77-96	92-115	100-125
25	57-71	63-78	70-87	84-105	100-125	110-137
26	63-78	70-87	78-97	92-115	110-137	120-150
27	70-87	78-97	87-108	100-125	120-150	130-162
28	78-97	87-108	97-121	110-137	130-162	140-175
29	87-108	97-121	108-135	121-151	140-175	151-188
30	97-121	108-135	121-151	135-168	151-188	168-210
31	108-135	121-151	135-168	151-188	168-210	188-235
32	121-151	135-168	151-188	168-210	188-235	210-262
33	135-168	151-188	168-210	188-235	210-262	235-293
34	151-188	168-210	188-235	210-262	235-293	262-327
35	168-210	188-235	210-262	235-293	262-327	292-365
36	188-235	210-262	235-293	262-327	292-365	324-405
37	210-262	235-293	262-327	292-365	324-405	360-life
38	235-293	262-327	292-365	324-405	360-life	360-life
39	262-327	292-365	324-405	360-life	360-life	360-life
40	292-365	324-405	360-life	360-life	360-life	360-life
41	324-405	360-life	360-life	360-life	360-life	360-life
42	360-life	360-life	360-life	360-life	360-life	360-life
43	life	life	life	life	life	life

Zone D labels the block of rows 25–27 at the left margin.

#6 DID YOU KNOW THAT?

If you are indicted by the Feds for being a drug pusher, or stick-up kid they will ensure that the guidelines specify a "substantial term of imprisonment."

(A) for the fact that you committed an offense as part of a pattern of criminal conduct from which you derived your income. Another word for this is <u>criminal livelihood,</u> which means that the defendant derived income from the pattern of criminal conduct that in any 12-month period exceeding 2000 times the then existing hourly minimum wage under Federal law; and (B) the totality of circumstances shows that such criminal conduct was the defendant's <u>primary</u> occupation in that 12 months (e.g., the defendant engaged in criminal conduct rather than regular legitimate employments or the defendant's criminal conduct).

Terry T. Ruffin

This is crazy, right? But the truth to this matter is once the Feds are in your business, they are in it knee deep and gangsta with it at the same time!

#7 Did you know that?

If you get caught with a gun in your possession and you have at least three prior convictions for a violent felony or serious drug offense were both committed on occasions different from one another. You will be subject to what they call the grave digger 924-E enhancement Arm Career Criminal Act, which has been in effect since 1984. This enhancement allows the Feds to give you no less than a 15-year sentence. What I am saying is this, if you have a bad criminal history, you can get up to a life sentence. Actually, that is what the guidelines call for 15 years to life for the A.C.C.A. sentence structure. And check this out, the Feds can go all of the way back and use your juvenile record to career you out. So if you have been catching a lot of cases that have involved some sort of violence or serious dope cases and you have these type of convictions on your criminal history. Then if you get caught with a pistol in your possession or around your vicinity, you qualify for the Arm Career Criminal Act. And the Feds will pick up your case and hit you with a 922 (g) offense and the 924-E enhancement. Remember, the only way that they can Arm Career you out is you have to get the 922 (g) offense, which is firearm by felon. It is a lot of young men of color that are doing a 15-year sentence or better for just being in possession of a firearm. Don't be street ignorant. Stay away from the guns.

#8 Did you know that?

Conspiracy is not selling drugs but only an agreement and one overt action. For example: Cat calls Bird and asks to borrow his vehicle, Bird replies, "For what?" In return Cat says, "I got to run around the corner and make a play, but I will look out." Bird replies, "Come and get the keys to the car."

At the end of this writing Bird is currently residing in a Federal Holding (cage) facility facing a conspiracy charge and a sentence range of 0 to 20 years.

The scenario I just gave is as simple as that. The Feds can take that simple gesture of trying to help someone out and cause you to be indicted, convicted, and sentenced by the Feds.

#9 Did you know that?

If you are on parole for a felony, if the parole officer comes to your home and does a search. If they find a gun, even if it is in a lockbox or trigger guard anywhere in the home. Even if it is registered to someone that lives in the home, you are going to jail.

So don't play dumb, if there are weapons inside of the home where you reside, <u>read, listen, and pay attention,</u> even if the weapons are antique rifles, or pistols. They are going to charge you with possession of firearm by felon.

#10 Did you know that?

The Feds can put a GPS tracker on your vehicle, you don't even know it's there, until you get indicted for the case they are investigating you on. And check this out, it's legal and over 65% of Federal cases that a GPS tracker was used,

Terry T. Ruffin

helped the Feds to a speedy conviction. This technology is an ace in the hole for the Feds and a black eye for the street-ignorant felon, so check your whip (car), you just might be getting followed.

APPENDIX 3

WHERE TO LOOK TO BECOME A STREETWISE REFERENCE INFORMATION

If you would like to find some of the information concerning Federal criminal offenses, guidelines, case statues, and enhancements that I used for examples in this book, you can find from these following resources:

1. The Federal Sentence and Guidelines book (due to the constant changes of Federal laws the Feds revise this book every year)

2. Federal Criminal Code and Rules (this book is also revised yearly)

3. Black's Law Dictionary

4. The local library in your city/law department

5. Google

6. Social media, one in particular Facebook (once on this site don't be afraid to ask questions concerning your situation. You will be surprised who can help.)

7. A paralegal

8. A community college or law school that has eager students of criminal or civil law that can help you

9. A lawyer, most lawyers give you a free consultation

10. A felon, who is experienced in law as he should

A LETTER FROM THE AUTHOR

Irst of all, I would like to thank each of you for taking the time out of your busy schedule to read my book, *The definition of Street Ignorance.* What inspired me to write this book was the fact that I too was a victim of street ignorance. In 2014, I was charged with possession of firearm by felon, after the case went before a grand jury, it was dismissed due to the firearm not actually being in my possession. It was in the vehicle that I was driving and belonged to the owner. A year later I was indicted by the Feds on the same gun, but not only was I indicted for the gun all over again, which carried a sentence of 0 to 10 years. I was also enhanced with a 924- E, Arm Career criminal offense, which carried a sentence of 15 years to life, due to me having more than three felony convictions, on my criminal history record. A case came out shortly after my arrest with the Feds that dealt specifically with the residual clause of my priors which revealed that my predicates did not qualify as crimes of violence. Therefore the 924-E enhancement was dropped and I pled guilty to my original guidelines which carried only 30 months. But due to my past few brushes with the law, I was given a 40-month upward departure. Therefore, I was sentenced to 70 months in Federal prison.

If it wasn't for that new case that came out, I would have been doing a 188 months or better sentence. For riding with a registered pistol in the owner's vehicle. My situation along with numerous of other cases that I have read, and seen hands on from other inmates I was incarcerated with, is what compelled me to write *The definition of Street Ignorance.* Who would ever have thought that someone could get a life sentence for being in possession of a firearm and having a past criminal history? And check this out, you don't even have to touch it. It can just be around you in your vicinity. If the police find it and you got priors, your case can go Fed. No matter who you are, rich or poor, and yeah, it's some broke offenders in the Feds too. Society has the perception that if you go to the Feds, you were getting money. That's only a myth because the indigent list stays full in the Feds. All you have to do is be a felon, and you qualify for a Federal indictment.

Being street ignorant is the greatest enemy among the players of the streets. And if you don't know how much time you can get for what you may be into, or the type of friends or homies you really have when it comes to the Feds knocking at your door. Then you might want to fall back and reevaluate your situation. The Feds are trying to get you off of the streets for life, while the streets are trying to take your life. This is the reality of street life. We have heard it so many times, that we as a people of color need to wake up, and start thinking.

The prison recidivism rate is so high now in Federal prison, that some inmates look at the institution as their second home, or a home that they never had. They feel more comfortable in prison in which gives them the sense of escape to elude real-life responsibilities. To the street players, this is my plea to you. It's time to grow up and take back your rightful places in society as fathers, sons, mentors and pillars in your community. Knowledge is power, and this power will allow you to have stability in your life. If you are operating mentally out of anything else besides growth, then you

                Terry T. Ruffin

will continue to suffer from these definitions of street ignorance that are written in this book!

May your journey in life be enriched in all things.

One love, the author,

Terry "Goodbrutha" Ruffin

DOCUMENTS AND IMAGES

UNITED STATES DISTRICT COURT
FOR THE EASTERN DISTRICT OF NORTH CAROLINA

UNITED STATES OF AMERICA	)	
	)	
vs.	)	**PRESENTENCE INVESTIGATION REPORT**
	)	
	)	Docket No.: 0417 5:14CR00285D-001
TERRY TERICE RUFFIN	)	
	)	

Prepared for: The Honorable James C. Dever III
Chief U.S. District Judge

Prepared by: Jacqueline G. Leonard
Senior U.S. Probation Officer
Raleigh, NC
919-861-8698

Assistant U.S. Attorney
John H. Bennett
215 South Evans Street, Suite 206
Greenville, NC 27858
252-830-0335

Defense Counsel
Jennifer A. Dominguez
150 Fayetteville Street, Suite 450
Raleigh, NC 27601
919-856-4236

Sentence Date: May 26, 2016

Offense: **Count 1**:
Felon in Possession of a Firearm and Ammunition
18 U.S.C. § 922(g)(1), 18 U.S.C. § 924(e)(1)
Not more than 10 years imprisonment/$250,000 fine
Class C Felony

Release Status: Arrested and detained on related state charges from January 20, 2014, until released
on bond March 20, 2014. Arrested and detained federally on June 3, 2015.

Detainers: No detainers.

*Final Draft Presentence Report disqualifying me as a A.C.C.A offender
back to 0 to 10 year guidelines from a fire arm.*

158   Terry T. Ruffin

94.   **Adjustment for Obstruction of Justice:** None.   <u>0</u>

95.   **Adjusted Offense Level (Subtotal):**   <u>20</u>

96.   **Chapter Four Enhancement:** None.   <u>0</u>

97.   **Acceptance of Responsibility:** The defendant has clearly demonstrated acceptance of responsibility for the offense. Accordingly, the offense level is decreased by two levels. USSG §3E1.1(a).   <u>-2</u>

98.   **Acceptance of Responsibility:** The defendant has assisted authorities in the investigation or prosecution of the defendant's own misconduct by timely notifying authorities of the intention to enter a plea of guilty. Accordingly, the offense level is decreased by one additional level. USSG §3E1.1(b).   <u>-1</u>

99.   **Total Offense Level:**   <u>17</u>

PART E. SENTENCING OPTIONS

<u>Custody</u>

100.   **Statutory Provisions:** The maximum term of imprisonment is 10 years. 18 U.S.C. § 922(g)(1) and 18 U.S.C. § 924(e)(1).

101.   **Guideline Provisions:** Based upon a total offense level of 17 and a criminal history category of VI, the guideline imprisonment range is 51 months to 63 months.

<u>Impact of Plea Agreement</u>

102.   Pursuant to 1B1.3, all offense behavior has been incorporated within the count(s) of conviction. Therefore, the Plea Agreement had no impact upon the guideline calculations.

<u>Supervised Release</u>

103.   **Statutory Provisions:** The Court may impose a term of supervised release of not more than three years. 18 U.S.C. § 3583(b)(2).

104.   **Guideline Provisions:** Since the offense is a Class C Felony, the guideline range for a term of supervised release is 1 year to 3 years. USSG §5D1.2(a)(2).

<u>Probation</u>

105.   **Statutory Provisions:** The defendant is eligible for not less than one nor more than five years probation because the offense is a Class C Felony. 18 U.S.C. § 3561(c)(1). One of the following must be imposed as a condition of probation unless extraordinary circumstances exist: a fine, restitution, or community service.

106.   **Guideline Provisions:** Since the applicable guideline range is in Zone D of the Sentencing Table, the defendant is ineligible for probation. USSG §5B1.1, comment.(n.2).

Final Draft Presentence Report Continued.

Thomas P. McNamara
Federal Public Defender

G. Alan DuBois
First Assistant

Sherri R. Alspaugh
Chief Trial Attorney

Stephen C. Gordon
Chief Appellate Attorney

Joseph H. Craven
Senior Litigator

Phone   919-856-4236
Toll-Free   888-603-5571
Fax   919-856-4477
Website   http://nce.fd.org

Assistant Federal Public Defenders:
Sonya M. Allen
A. Robert Bell, III
Cindy J. Bembry
Lauren H. Brennan
Eric J. Brignac
Jennifer A. Dominguez
Devon L. Donahue
Marshall H. Ellis
Joseph B. Gilbert
Ormond Harriott
Suzanne Little
Christopher J. Locascio
James A. Martin
Diana H. Pereira
Joseph L. Ross, II
Katherine Shea
James E. Todd, Jr.
Susan M. Umstead
Edwin C. Walker
Robert E. Waters

Office of the Federal Public Defender

150 Fayetteville Street, Suite 450
Raleigh, North Carolina 27601

July 24, 2015

Terry Ruffin
Legal Mail
Albemarle District Jail
210 Executive Dr. S
Elizabeth City, NC 27909

Dear Mr. Ruffin:

Thanks for your letter I received today. I received your previous letter as well. Please just hang in there. I know this is a stressful time for you. We are trying first to do extensive research to see if you will be classified as an Armed Career Criminal. I have a research attorney working on this as we speak. As we discussed at our meeting, that is the single most important thing to determine.

I have also reached out to the prosecutor when I was asking the court to continue (or move) your court date. In that discussion, she sounded like she might consider alternative charges to the felon in possession charge if we determine that you are an Armed Career Criminal. For instance, in a case like yours I might ask her to consider possession of a stolen firearm as you were not. She didn't say anything definitive and I didn't ask her to commit (not at this stage), but I am hopeful that she is not out to get you. So, hang in there. I know there is confusion, but that is because this new case is going to cause changes in the offenses used to make some an Armed Career Criminal and we need to ride this out.

Your arraignment is now set for October 13, 2015. I hope to see you sometime in early August to give you some sort of update on the research. I look forward to hearing from your family. If I don't hear from them soon, I can reach out to them as well in a few weeks. But this next week or two I am immersed in a motions hearing preparation for another client. Until I see you, take care.

Sincerely,

Letter from lawyer telling me to hang in there concerning A.C.C.A.

160   Terry T. Ruffin

Thomas P. McNamara
Federal Public Defender

G. Alan DuBois
First Assistant

Sherri R. Alspaugh
Chief Trial Attorney

Stephen C. Gordon
Chief Appellate Attorney

Joseph H. Craven
Senior Litigator

Joseph B. Gilbert
Chief Training Attorney

Phone   919-856-4236
Toll-Free 888-603-5571
Fax   919-856-4477
Website   http://nce.fd.org

Office of the Federal Public Defender
150 Fayetteville Street, Suite 450
Raleigh, North Carolina 27601

Assistant Federal Public Defenders:
Sonya M. Allen
A. Robert Bell, III
Cindy J. Bembry
Lauren H. Brennan
Eric J. Brignac
Jennifer A. Dominguez
Devon L. Donahue
Marshall H. Ellis
Ormond Harriott
Suzanne Little
Christopher J. Locascio
James A. Martin
Diana H. Pereira
Joseph L. Ross, II
Katherine Shea
James E. Todd, Jr.
Susan M. Umstead
Edwin C. Walker
Robert E. Waters

October 28, 2015

Terry T. Ruffin #18569-057
Legal Mail
Albemarle District Jail
210 Executive Dr. S.
Elizabeth City, NC 27909

Dear Terry:

I just wanted to give you an update to let you know that I haven't forgotten about you. I had a number of conversations with the prosecutor in your case trying to get you a different plea – one to possession of a stolen firearm. This is because I want to avoid the risk of you being considered an armed career criminal at sentencing and then having a mandatory minimum sentence of 15 years. As we have discussed extensively, a lot of your priors have the potential of being armed career criminal predicates and others might be taken off that predicate list by the rationale in the *U.S. v. Johnson* case.

The initial response from her has been that she will not offer you that plea. So, I've been waiting to have a meeting with her and her boss to try to convince them in person to give you that plea. I have that meeting today and I will report back once I have a clear understanding of whether they will deliver a stolen firearm plea or not. Hang in there.

Sincerely,

Letter from lawyer trying to get alternative plea to avoid A.C.C.A enhancement.

5:14-CR-285-1-D

TERRY TONLE RUFFIN
210 S. EXECUTIVE dr.
ELIZABETH City, N.C. 27909

①

150 Fayetteville Street, Suite 450
Raleigh, North Carolina 27601

March 13, 2016

Dear Mrs

    I am writing you in reference to a few concerns that I have pertaining to my sentencing process. On our meeting on the March 10. You spoke in such a way that confused me a little. I have put alot of my time here in this place studying and researching the 924-E ACCA as well as other issues such as Residual Clause, and Categorical Approach language, as well as the Supreme Court findings pertaining to definitions of Violent Felonies, And from my findings Physical force definitely requires "Purposeful, Violent and Aggressive. A force that must be Characteristic of the enumerated offenses. The Supreme Court in Johnson v. United States not only struck down the residual clause in offenses that were considered to be violent. but identified clearly what type of predicates could be used to Career a federal defendant out. The 1998 conviction of Attempt Robbery that I have in Washington, D.C. Should not even be a predicate because there was no form of violence in the offence And it was without force and under D.C. Code Ann § 22-2901 U.S vs. Mobley. I know that you say nothing has changed. but if my motion was to buy additional time to continue plea negotiations

Letter to lawyer from me relating to my concerns during the fight for my life!

Terry T. Ruffin

with the government. How did the Johnson Case affect my Case? If all I keep hearing that i'm still an ACCA Candidate? You stated that WE WERE going to be doing Alot of fighting my Predicates. But how can we Fight when you say that I have a Judge thats not hearing it? By all MEANS I FEEL that this is NOT FAIR FOR ME Concerning my Case. There are defendants going in Front of Federal Judges such As Judge Howard And Judge Boyle with shooting Charges where victims were hurt And Robbery Charges That were not Considered to be violent due to The Residual Clause. No one was hurt or harmed in any of my offenses but i'm still a Candidate. Is there Anyway that WE Can File An Updated Sentencing memo to have with us during Sentencing Just in Case.

There is not A day that goes by that i'm NOT stressing this Fact. I Just pray that all works out on our behalf. I FEEL trapped. I Also had my Family to Correct the spelling of Judge Dever name on the Character letters And to resend them to you. My Faith is big Just wanna be sure that your Also being optimistic with me. I believe in Miracles!

As I Always tell you I Am grateful to have you As my Attorney And I Know that God will Prevail! Please hear my cry And thanks for all that you do. And I Am Fully Prepared to Speak with Judge Dever when time presents.

Sincerely

P.S. Can you please File And send me A Copy Back. Thanks
Be Blessed.

Continued.

ADDENDUM TO THE PRESENTENCE REPORT

UNITED STATES DISTRICT COURT
FOR THE EASTERN DISTRICT OF NORTH CAROLINA
UNITED STATES V. TERRY TERICE RUFFIN, DKT. 0417 5:14CR00285D-001

OBJECTIONS

Legal and Guideline Applications

▸1. **Paragraph 90**: Ruffin objects to his base offense level being calculated at 20. He does not believe he has a scoreable felony conviction of either a crime of violence or a controlled substance offense for purposes of 2K2.1(a)(2). He asserts that the base offense level of 20 is predicated on a prior conviction for "Second Degree Kidnapping" and "Common Law Robbery." His correct base offense level should be 14 as defined by USSG §4B1.2.

This is the case because neither of these crimes, have "as an element the use, attempted use, or threatened use of physical force against the person of another." *See State v. Sturdivant*, 304 N.C. 293, 283 S.E.2d 719, 729 (1981) ("[North Carolina] kidnaping can be just as effectively accomplished by fraudulent means as by the use of force, threats, or intimidation"); *United States v. Carmichael*, 408 F. App'x 769, 770 (4th Cir. 2011) (unpublished) ("[Common Law Robbery] does not necessarily have 'as an element the use, attempted use, or threatened use of physical force against the person of another,' § 924(e)(2)(B)(i), and is not 'burglary, arson, or extortion, [. . . and does not] involve[] use of explosives.'").

Additionally, none of the two potential predicate crimes are "burglary of a dwelling, arson, or extortion, [or] involves the use of explosives." The Supreme Court's May 2, 2016 decision in *Ocasio v. United States*, 578 U.S. ___ (2016), coupled with its prior holding in *Descamps v. United States*, 133 S. Ct. 2276 (2013), decisively precludes to any argument that North Carolina common law robbery should be classified as generic "extortion," and thus fall within the enumerated crimes. In *Descamps*, the Supreme Court stated that whenever there is a "mismatch in elements" between a generic, enumerated offense under the ACCA and a state predicate crime, the state predicate crime cannot ever constitute the generic offense for purposes of the ACCA enhancement. *Descamps*, 133 S. Ct. At 2292. That is precisely the case as between generic extortion and North Carolina common law robbery, since extortion requires, as an element, that the taking of the victim's property be *consensual, see* North Carolina Pattern Jury Instructions 217.10 (stating that the third element of North Carolina common law robbery is "that the other person did not *voluntarily consent* to the taking and carrying away of the property."). In fact, the Supreme Court noted in *Ocascio* that consent is what distinguishes a Hobbs Act extortion from a robbery. *Ocascio*, 578 U.S. at ___, slip op. At 15 ("As used in the Hobbs Act, the phrase 'with his consent' is designed to distinguish extortion . . . from robbery . . . .").

Objections against my predicated prevailing that the residual clause was
unconstitutionally vague under the Johnson Case.

164   Terry T. Ruffin

Finally, the commentary in the guidelines at application note 1 – specifically its mention that crime of violence includes kidnaping and robbery – does not change defendant's argument that these are not crimes of violence post-*Johnson*. Guideline commentary is authoritative but only if it is not inconsistent with the actual language of the guideline itself—which at all times remains controlling. *Stinson v. United States*, 508 U.S. 36, 38 (1993). Put another way, commentary may illuminate or illustrate a guideline's language but it may not expand its scope or alter its meaning. *Shell*, 789 F.3d at 345 ("§ 4B1.2 provides a separate two-part definition of crime of violence in its text, with the commentary serving only to amplify that definition, and any inconsistency between the two resolved in favor of the text").

Prior to *Johnson*, with § 4B1.2(a)(2)'s residual clause intact, the commentary including kidnaping and robbery as crimes of violence was not inconsistent with the language of the guideline. It simply reflected the Sentencing Commission's determination that robbery and kidnaping "otherwise involve[d] conduct that presents a serious potential risk of physical injury to another." Indeed, this is precisely the conclusion reached by the Supreme Court when analyzing this same note's inclusion of attempt offenses within the crime of violence definition:

This judgment was based on the Commission's review of empirical sentencing data and presumably reflects an assessment that attempt crimes often pose a similar risk of injury as completed offenses. *James*, 550 U.S. at 206 (emphasis supplied). In other words, the application note is essentially just a list of offenses the Commission believed fell within the residual clause. It does not, and indeed could not, reflect a freestanding determination, detached from the actual language of § 4B1.2, that these offenses independently qualify as crimes of violence. *See United States v. Armijo*, 651 F.3d 1226, 1236-37 (10th Cir. 2011) (application note listing manslaughter as a crime of violence could not trump Guideline language limiting crime of violence predicate to offenses involving intentional conduct); *see also Shell*, 789 F.3d at 345-46 (holding application note listing "forcible sex offense" as a crime of violence did not qualify rape conviction as a predicate where that conviction did not satisfy crime of violence definition contained in guideline text). Now that the Supreme Court has struck down the residual clause as unconstitutionally vague, any application note purporting to define its reach or enumerate its contents is simply irrelevant. That said, neither second degree kidnaping nor common law robbery are crimes of violence post-*Johnson*.

<u>Probation Officer's Response</u>: Pursuant to USSG §2K2.1(a)(4)(A), the base offense level is 20 if the defendant committed any part of the instant offense subsequent to sustaining one felony conviction of either a crime of violence or a controlled substance offense. USSG §4B1.2(a)(1) defines a "crime of violence" as any offense under federal or state law, punishable by imprisonment for a term exceeding one year, that (1) has an element the use, attempted use, or threatened use of physical force against the person of another, or (2) is burglary of a dwelling, arson, or extortion, involves use of explosives, or otherwise involves conduct that presents a serious potential risk of physical injury to another. In the case-at-bar, the defendant has been convicted of Common Law Robbery. Pursuant to NCGS §§14-87.1 and 14-87, a person commits common law robbery when any person or persons unlawfully take or attempt to take personal property from another or from any

Continued.

The definition of Street Ignorance 165

clause" of the ACCA, finding it "unconstitutionally vague." <u>Johnson</u>, however, does not address what constitutes a "crime of violence" for guideline purposes. While the Fourth Circuit previously observed that the ACCA definition for "violent felony" and the guideline definition for "crime of violence" are virtually identical, the Fourth Circuit, at this time, has not specifically addressed if <u>Johnson</u> is applicable to the guideline residual clause. Furthermore, Application Note 1 of the commentary to USSG §4B1.2 includes additional enumerated offenses beyond those listed in ACCA, including robbery. Based on these reasons, the probation officer contends the defendant committed the instant offense subsequent to sustaining a felony conviction for a crime of violence, and the base offense level is 20.

Until further guidance is received from the Fourth Circuit, the probation office will continue to use the guidelines residual clause, if appropriate, to enhance a defendant's sentence. However, should the court sustain this objection, the adjusted offense level will be 14, the Total Offense Level will be 12, the advisory guideline imprisonment range will be 30 to 37 months, and the advisory guideline fine range will be $3,000 to $30,000.

Respectfully Submitted,

/s/ Jacqueline G. Leonard
Senior U.S. Probation Officer

Approved:

/s/ Jay F. Neely
Supervising U.S. Probation Officer

5/19/2016 3:20 PM

Continued.

                    Terry T. Ruffin

UNITED STATES DISTRICT COURT
FOR THE EASTERN DISTRICT OF NORTH CAROLINA

UNITED STATES OF AMERICA	)	
	)	
vs.	)	**PRESENTENCE INVESTIGATION REPORT**
	)	
	)	**Docket No.:** 0417 5:14CR00285D-001
TERRY TERICE RUFFIN	)	
	)	

Prepared for: The Honorable James C. Dever III
Chief U.S. District Judge

Prepared by: Jacqueline G. Leonard
Senior U.S. Probation Officer
Raleigh, NC
919-861-8698

Assistant U.S. Attorney	**Defense Counsel**
Jane J. Jackson	Jennifer A. Dominguez
310 New Bern Avenue, Suite 800	150 Fayetteville Street, Suite 450
Raleigh, NC 27601-1461	Raleigh, NC 27601
919-856-4292	919-856-4236

Sentence Date: April 18, 2016

Offense: <u>Count 1</u>:
Felon in Possession of a Firearm and Ammunition
18 U.S.C. § 922(g)(1), 18 U.S.C. § 924(e)(1)
15 years to life imprisonment/$250,000 fine
Class A Felony   *Object*

Release Status: Arrested and detained on related state charges from January 20, 2014, until released
on bond on March 20, 2014. Arrested and detained on federally on June 3, 2015.

Detainers: No detainers.

*First pre-sentence report qualifying me as a A.C.C.A offender. 15 years
to life for a firearm.*

The definition of Street Ignorance   167

90. **Specific Offense Characteristics:** None.   <u>0</u>

91. **Victim Related Adjustment:** None.   <u>0</u>

92. **Adjustment for Role in the Offense:** None.   <u>0</u>

93. **Adjustment for Obstruction of Justice:** None.   <u>0</u>

94. **Adjusted Offense Level (Subtotal):**   <u>24</u>

95. **Chapter Four Enhancement:** The offense of conviction is a violation of 18 U.S.C. § 922(g), and the defendant has at least three prior convictions for a violent felony or serious drug offense, or both, which were committed on different occasions. Therefore, the defendant is an armed career criminal and subject to an enhanced sentence under the provisions of 18 U.S.C. § 924(e). The offense level is 33. USSG §4B1.4.   <u>33</u>

96. **Acceptance of Responsibility:** The defendant has clearly demonstrated acceptance of responsibility for the offense. Accordingly, the offense level is decreased by two levels. USSG §3E1.1(a).   <u>-2</u>

97. **Acceptance of Responsibility:** The defendant has assisted authorities in the investigation or prosecution of the defendant's own misconduct by timely notifying authorities of the intention to enter a plea of guilty. Accordingly, the offense level is decreased by one additional level. USSG §3E1.1(b).   <u>-1</u>

98. **Total Offense Level:**   <u>30</u>

PART E. SENTENCING OPTIONS

Custody

99. **Statutory Provisions:** The minimum term of imprisonment is 15 years and the maximum term is life. 18 U.S.C. § 922(g)(1) and 18 U.S.C. § 924(e)(1).

100. **Guideline Provisions:** Based upon a total offense level of 30 and a criminal history category of VI, the guideline imprisonment range is 168 months to 210 months. However, the statutorily authorized minimum sentence of 15 years is greater than the minimum of the guideline range; therefore, the guideline range is 180 months to 210 months. USSG §5G1.1(c)(2).

Impact of Plea Agreement

101. Pursuant to 1B1.3, all offense behavior has been incorporated within the count(s) of conviction. Therefore, the Plea Agreement had no impact upon the guideline calculations.

Continued.

Terry T. Ruffin

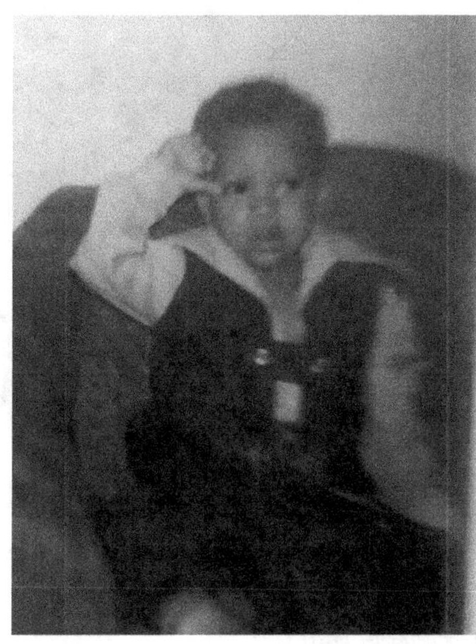

Age 2
Baltimore, Maryland. 1971

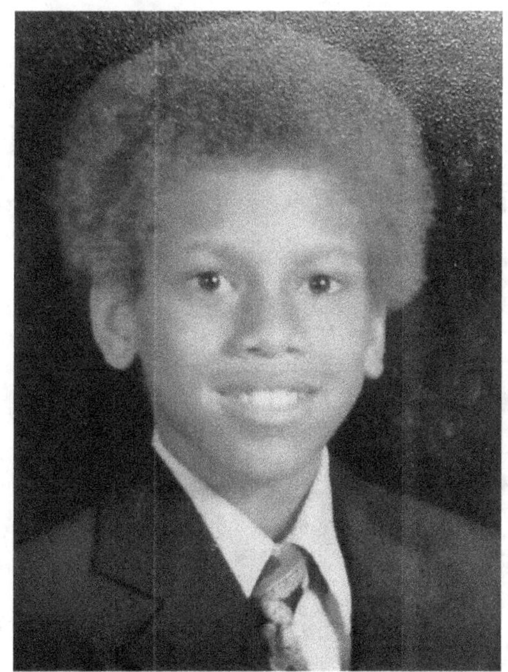

Me. 1975

Me and my brother Quentin. 1977

Stepdad, me, brother and mom. 1978

Terry T. Ruffin

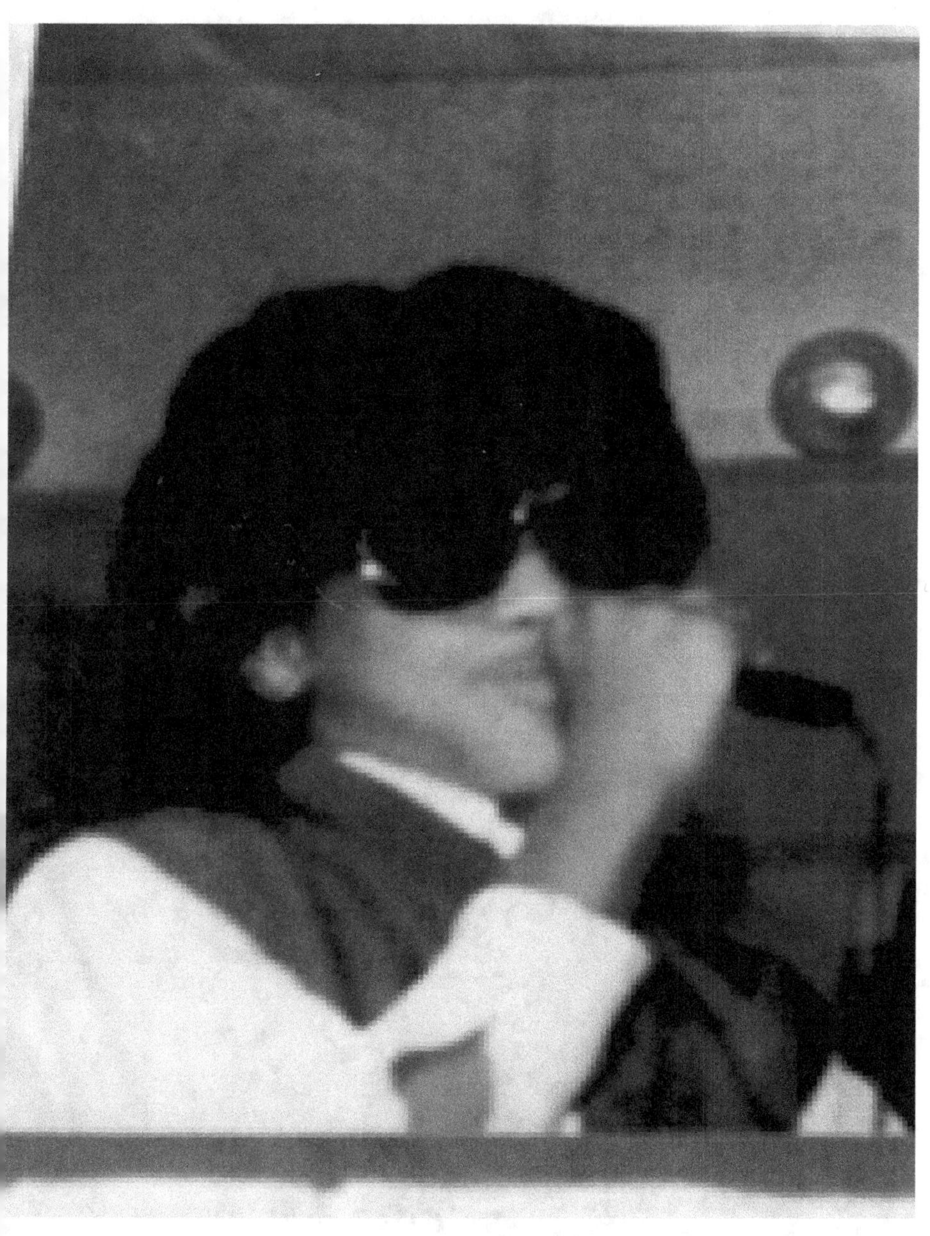

Putting on the Hits competition; Sports World; Rocky Mount, N.C. 1984

Me and my daughter Lasheena. Christmas. 1994

*Me in New Jersey
grabbing pizza pies.
2002*

Terry T. Ruffin

N.C. Community College Food Service Technology Program.
N.C.D.C. 2005

North Carolina Dept. of Labor Apprenticeship program.
2006

In studio Queen City. 2008

Yella-Rain performs for the Council of the Blind Benefit. 2011

 Terry T. Ruffin

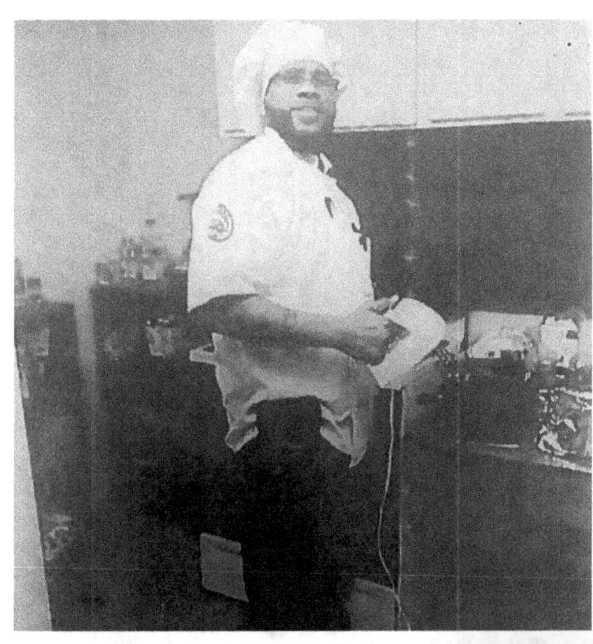

Me preparing Boys and Girls Club meal. 2014

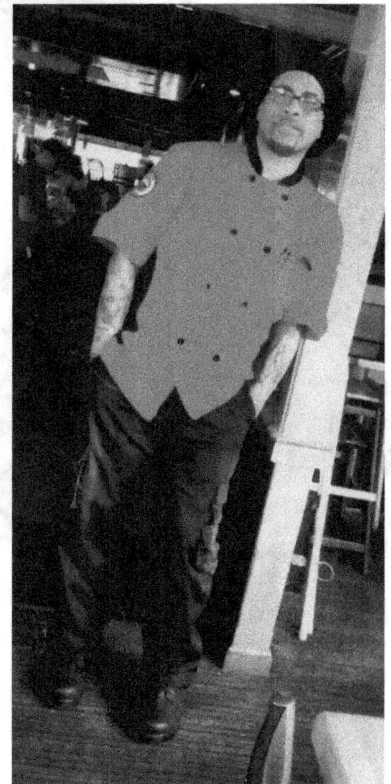

Me at work. 2020

Me at Life Change Ministries in Wilmington, N.C. 2020

 Terry T. Ruffin